First World War
and Army of Occupation
War Diary
France, Belgium and Germany

24 DIVISION
Divisional Troops
Machine Gun Corps
24 Battalion
5 March 1918 - 30 May 1919

WO95/2201/2

The Naval & Military Press Ltd
www.nmarchive.com
Published in association with The National Archives

Published by

The Naval & Military Press Ltd

Unit 10 Ridgewood Industrial Park,

Uckfield, East Sussex,

TN22 5QE England

Tel: +44 (0) 1825 749494

www.naval-military-press.com

www.nmarchive.com

This diary has been reprinted in facsimile from the original. Any imperfections are inevitably reproduced and the quality may fall short of modern type and cartographic standards.

© **Crown Copyright**
Images reproduced by permission of The National Archives, London, England, 2015.

Contents

Document type	Place/Title	Date From	Date To
Heading	WO95/2201-2		
Heading	BEF 24 Division Troops 24 Bn Machine Gun Corps 1918 Mar-1919 May		
War Diary	Devise	05/03/1918	11/03/1918
War Diary	Vraignes	12/03/1918	22/03/1918
War Diary	Brie	22/03/1918	23/03/1918
War Diary	Lihons	23/03/1918	25/03/1918
War Diary	Puzeau	25/03/1918	26/03/1918
War Diary	Warvillers	28/03/1918	28/03/1918
War Diary	Bois De Senecat	28/03/1918	01/04/1918
War Diary	Thezy Glimont	02/04/1918	04/04/1918
War Diary	Bois-De Centelles	04/04/1918	04/04/1918
War Diary	Saleux	06/04/1918	06/04/1918
War Diary	St Valery	07/04/1918	09/04/1918
War Diary	Sallenelle	10/04/1918	17/04/1918
War Diary	Belval	18/04/1918	18/04/1918
War Diary	Conteville	19/04/1918	30/04/1918
Heading	War Diary Of 24th Battn M.G.C. From 1.5.18 To 31.5.18		
War Diary	Les Brebis	01/05/1918	31/05/1918
Heading	War Diary Of 24th Battn M.G.C. From 1.6.18 To 30.6.18 (Volume 3)		
War Diary	Les Brebis	01/06/1918	30/06/1918
Map			
Heading	War Diary Of 24th Battn. M.G.C. From 1.7.18 to 31.7.18 (Volume 4)		
War Diary	Les Brebis	01/07/1918	31/07/1918
Heading	War Diary Of 24th Battn M.G.C. From 1.8.18 To 31.8.18 Volume 6		
War Diary	Les Brebis	01/08/1918	31/08/1918
Heading	War Diary of 24th Battalion Machine Gun Corps. From 1/9/18 to 30/9/18 (Volume)		
War Diary	Fosse 11 (Les Brebis)	01/09/1918	28/09/1918
War Diary	Maisnilles Ruitz	29/09/1918	29/09/1918
War Diary	Maisnilles	29/09/1918	29/09/1918
War Diary	Bouquemaison	30/09/1918	30/09/1918
War Diary	Coullemont	30/09/1918	30/09/1918
Map			
Heading	War Diary of 24th Battn M.G.C. From 1.10.18 To 31.10.18 (Volume 7)		
War Diary	Coullemont	01/10/1918	06/10/1918
War Diary	Lock 6 Canal Du Nord	07/10/1918	07/10/1918
War Diary	West Of Cantaing	07/10/1918	07/10/1918
War Diary	West Of Rumilly	08/10/1918	09/10/1918
War Diary	Awoingt	09/10/1918	10/10/1918
War Diary	Rieux Tower	10/10/1918	11/10/1918
War Diary	Outskirts Of Avesnes	11/10/1918	11/10/1918
War Diary	Avesnes	12/10/1918	12/10/1918
War Diary	W. Outskirts of St. Aubert	12/10/1918	14/10/1918
War Diary	St. Aubert	15/10/1918	17/10/1918

War Diary	East Outskirts of Cambrai	18/10/1918	25/10/1918
War Diary	St Aubert	26/10/1918	31/10/1918
Map			
Map	Air-Line Junctions Telephone Office or Centre		
Map			
Heading	War Diary Of 24th Battn M.G.C. From 1.11.18 To 30.11.18 Volume 8		
War Diary	St Aubert	01/11/1918	01/11/1918
War Diary	St Martin	02/11/1918	02/11/1918
War Diary	Sepmeries	03/11/1918	03/11/1918
War Diary	Maresches	03/11/1918	04/11/1918
War Diary	Le Corons	04/11/1918	05/11/1918
War Diary	Le Bois Crette	05/11/1918	07/11/1918
War Diary	Bavay	07/11/1918	07/11/1918
War Diary	Longueville	08/11/1918	09/11/1918
War Diary	Feignes	09/11/1918	10/12/1918
War Diary	Bavay	10/12/1918	16/12/1918
War Diary	Wargnies-Le-Petit	17/12/1918	17/12/1918
War Diary	Denain	18/12/1918	18/12/1918
War Diary	Aniche	19/11/1918	25/11/1918
War Diary	Sameon	26/11/1918	30/11/1918
Miscellaneous	D.A.A.G. 24th. Division.	05/03/1919	05/03/1919
Heading	24 Battn G Corps Vol 10		
War Diary	Sameon	01/12/1918	18/12/1918
War Diary	Tournai	20/12/1918	31/12/1918
War Diary	The D.A.G. 3rd Echelon.	01/03/1919	01/03/1919
Heading	War Diary For The Month Of January 1919 Volume No.10		
War Diary	Tournai	01/01/1919	30/01/1919
Heading	War Diary For Month Of February 1919		
War Diary	Tournai	01/02/1919	28/02/1919
Miscellaneous	D.A.G. G.H.Q. 3rd Echelon.	03/04/1919	03/04/1919
Heading	24th Battalion Machine Gun Corps War Diary For The Month Of March 1919 Volume 13		
War Diary	Tournai	01/03/1919	14/03/1919
War Diary	Tournai	01/03/1919	23/03/1919
War Diary	Tournai	15/03/1919	26/03/1919
War Diary	Marquain	27/03/1919	31/03/1919
War Diary	Tournai	24/03/1919	26/03/1919
War Diary	Marquain	27/03/1919	31/03/1919
Heading	War Diary For The Month Of April 1919 Volume 13		
War Diary	Marquain	01/04/1919	12/04/1919
War Diary	Marquain	01/04/1919	30/04/1919
War Diary	Marquain	13/04/1919	30/04/1919
Heading	War Diary for Month of May 1919		
Heading	24th Div Group		
War Diary	Marquain	01/05/1919	30/05/1919

W095/22012

BEF

24 DIVISION TROOPS

24 BN MACHINE GUN CORPS

1918 MAR — 1919 MAY

WAR DIARY
or
INTELLIGENCE SUMMARY.

(Erase heading not required.)

24 Bn M.G Corps

Place	Date	Hour	Summary of Events and Information	Remarks and references to Appendices
DEVISE	5.3.18		The No 24 Battalion, Machine Gun Corps, was formed on this day, consisting of 17th 72nd 73rd and 191st Machine Gun Companies. Headquarters of the Battalion to composed as follows:-	The 17th 72nd 73rd and 191st M.G. Coys concentrated at DEVISE on the 5th April, and remained there until the 11th April.

Officer Commanding ... Lieut. Colonel N.I. WHITTY D.S.O
2nd in Command ... Major G.H. STAMPE
Adjutant ... Lieut. P.M. ANDREWS
Transport Officer ... 2nd Lt. W.H. ROGERS
Signalling Officer ... To be appointed
Medical Officer ... Do
Quartermaster ... Hon Lieut. A. VICKERY

The following Machine Gun Companies are incorporated to form the Battalion:-

17th M.G. Coy. to become 'A' Coy. Sections 1 - 4
72nd M.G. Coy. " 'B' Coy. " 5 - 8
73rd M.G. Coy. " 'C' Coy. " 9 - 12
191st M.G. Coy " 'D' Coy. " 13 - 16

The Companies will be Commanded as follows:-

'A' Coy. Major J. JOYCE M.C.
'B' " Capt. R. DARBY
'C' " Capt. J.B. GAWTHORPE
'D' " Capt. R. GREEN

WAR DIARY
or
INTELLIGENCE SUMMARY.
(Erase heading not required.)

Army Form C. 2118.

Place	Date	Hour	Summary of Events and Information	Remarks and references to Appendices
	9.3.18		Lieut. Col. W.I. Whitty D.S.O. took command of the Battalion	
	10.3.18		2 Companies of the Battalion moved from Devise and relieved the dismounted division in the line Jeancourt – Le Verguier – Vadencourt – Maissemy.	
	11.3.18		Remaining 2 Companies moved from Devise and completed the above relief at 9.30 p.m.	
Vraignes	12.3.18		Battalion H.Q. moved to Vraignes.	
	13.3.18		5 O.R's reported to the Battn from Infantry Base Battalions	
	14.3.18		15 O.R's reported to the Battn from Base.	
	15.3.18		7702 R.S.M. Dare R. reported to this Battn for duty. Hon. Lieut. Q.M. A. Vickery joined the Battn.	
	16.3.18		2nd Lieut. W.D. Rogers appointed Assistant Transport Officer	
			6 O.R's reported as reinforcements from the Base	
	20.3.18		44 O.R's reported from Infantry Base Battalions	
			14 R.K. Signallers attached for duty from the 24th Div. Sig. Coy.	
	21.3.18		The 24th Machine Gun Battn. relieving the line Jeancourt – Le Verguier – Vadencourt	
Maissemy		4.20 am	Enemy opened heavy bombardment on our entire front.	
		5.5 "	This was reported to Div. H.Q	
		6.30 "	Heard from Div. H.Q. S.O.S. had gone up on our right.	
		5.52 "	Ordered by Div. H.Q's to man Battle Stations	

Army Form C. 2118.

WAR DIARY
or
INTELLIGENCE SUMMARY.
(Erase heading not required.)

Place	Date	Hour	Summary of Events and Information	Remarks and references to Appendices
VRAIGNES.	21.3.16	6.32am	Shelling of Back Areas increased, also our own Artillery	
		7.30am	66th Divn on left report S.O.S. gone up and fighting in progress	
		10.10am	MAJOR STAMPE proceeded to SMALLFOOT WOOD to establish advanced H.Q (C. Coy.)	
		12 Noon	2nd LIEUT. WEBB wounded.	
		2.9pm	Div. H.Q. believes that MAISEMY is holding out. COOKER QUARRY believed to be occupied by the RIFLE BRIGADE. Gun in HILL SPINNEY holding out. 2 M.G's in R3 CENTRAL and 2 M.G's in L29A and L29C and holding out (MAP REF 62c 1-100,000)	
		2.50pm	Wire sent to D.A.D.O.S asking for 4 Vickers guns & tripods	

WAR DIARY
INTELLIGENCE SUMMARY

Place	Date	Hour	Summary of Events and Information	Remarks and references to Appendices
VRAIGNES	21.3.18	3.30 p.m.	Report received from Div. H.Q that at 2 p.m. 2 M.G's were in action at L 28 Central. 2 M.G's in the LE VERGUIER SWITCH, 2 M.G's in HILL SPINNEY, 2 M.G's at R.8d. 8, 4. 2 M.G's in R.9b. 8.2 (Map 62c 1-100,000)	
		4.30 p.m.	2 M.G's and 1 Spare M.G placed in position covering an approach to JEANCOURT moved by 17th I.B. to VIXEN REDOUBT and were in action there for the rest of the day. (MAP 62c 1-100,000)	
		6.20 p.m.	Report by 2nd Lieut. BAMLET "C" Coy at 3 p.m. "C" Coy's H.Q moved back to approximately the BROWN LINE East of BÉHICOURT o/c "C" Coy. reported to MIDDLESEX H.Q. VIPER REDOUBT to find out where guns were most required. 72nd BRIGADE had retired; the brigades at MASSEMY were destroyed; a counter attack was made, on the left and the centre kilto. At 2 p.m; Artillery Major reported enemy fallen slightly from MAISSEMY; 72nd BDE H.Q moved forward again to Rd position at VERMAND	
		6.30 p.m.	o/c "A" Coy. reports all guns still holding out, excepting guns which retired from APPLETREE Rd. to PYEUMEL COPSE.	
		7 p.m.	CPL JACKMAN "C" Coy. brought his gun back from GAUBRIERS WOOD being sole survivor of his team. and reported enemy occupation of whole of wood.	
		7.30 p.m.	Report received that LE VERGUIER still holding out.	
		8 p.m.	2 M.G's of "C" Coy located at 72nd BDE H.Q in VERMAND	
		9 p.m.	1 M.G and 2nd Lieut. PERCHEY located in trench E. of BEHICOURT.	

WAR DIARY
INTELLIGENCE SUMMARY
(Erase heading not required.)

Army Form C. 2118.

Place	Date	Hour	Summary of Events and Information	Remarks and references to Appendices
VRAIGNES.	21-3-18	11 p.m.	2ND LIEUT. MCINTYRE "C" Coy located with 4 guns in LEVERGUIER SWITCH	
		11:30 p.m.	1 Gun of "C" Coy located in VIXEN REDOUBT enemy reported to be in APPLE TREE WALK	
		11:45 p.m.	2/CPL from "D" Coy. reports that CAPT DARBY was wounded about 2 p.m. also LIEUT. KAY about that time.	
	22.3.18	1 am.	Message from MAJOR STAMPE:- Am OTH with 17th I.B. but if possible I want to try to find "C" Coy. lost during the night. "A" Coy. apparent alright, and LEVERGUIER is still holding out. VADENCOURT CHATEAU now in hands of the enemy.	
			Report received from O.C. "A" Coy:- Formed strong point at L.32.C.99.70 with 2 M.G's 4 Lewis Guns, 100 men and 2 Heavy Trench mortars	
		5 am.	Line held R.28 Central - R.22.C.27 - R.22.C.45 - R.15 Central - R.9.a.8.9 R.9.a.99 MAP - 62D - 1-100,000 R.3 Central W of THIERRY COPSE and include LEVERGUIER by acute salient S. of PLEUMEL COPSE to JEANCOURT which is just included and N.W to HESBECOURT (Message from MAJOR STAMPE)	
		8 am.	2ND LIEUT DOUGLAS reported to Bn. H.Q. to arrange to And belts to 2 M.G's at VERMAND and 2 Guns under 2ND LIEUT PERCHEY at BEHICOURT. 2ND LIEUT. DOUGLAS states that situation at 6.30 am was normal, but the bombardment continued on the left.	

Army Form C. 2118.

WAR DIARY
or
INTELLIGENCE SUMMARY
(Erase heading not required.)

Place	Date	Hour	Summary of Events and Information	Remarks and references to Appendices
	22.3.18	11 am	2ND LIEUT. DEWHIRST and Section of 4 Gunners moved from VRAIGNES and reported to C.O of the Cavalry, afterwards receiving instructions to take up position in the GREEN LINE, again returning to the line he took up position in a line W of POEUILLY where he stayed in position until CAPT. GREEN who joined him during the evening of the 22nd; received instructions to evacuate that line at 3 am on the 23rd and take up new positions in a line W of the CROSS ROADS at ESTREES. The retirement returned during the morning of the 23rd through DEVISE & ATHIES until the rivers was crossed at ST CHRIST.	W.B.

WAR DIARY
or
INTELLIGENCE SUMMARY

Army Form C. 2118.

Place	Date	Hour	Summary of Events and Information	Remarks and references to Appendices
VRAIGNES	22.3.18	11.35am	Message from "D" Coy: "I am moving up to SMALLFOOT WOOD with 8 O.R's of "D" Co. and 1 man of "A" Coy, have 1 gun complete and I left boxes who driven out of LEVERGUIER early this morning; believe that all other gun teams of "D" Coy have been captured, have been unable to get in touch with O/C's "A" & "D" Coys. Have just reported to B.H.Q 73rd INF. BDE Signed H.H. ROBINSON 2nd LIEUT.	
		12 NOON	The Battn fell back, fighting through the 50th Divn. who were occupying the GREEN LINE - BERNES - FLECHIN - POEUILLY - CAULINCOURT (after receiving order from DIV. H.Q at BRIE) Moving North of VERMAND - BRIE Road	
BRIE.	22/23 3/18		The Battn concentrated at BRIE during the night of the 22nd 23rd 2ND LT. GORDON reported wounded and missing on the 21st "B" Coy 2ND LT. HANCOCK reported missing on the 21st "B" Coy 2ND LT. WILLIAMS reported missing on the 21st "B" Coy 2ND LT. HOLT reported missing on the 21st "C" Coy MAJOR JOYCE "A" Coy reported wounded on the 22nd 2ND LT. PARSONS "A" Coy reported wounded on the 22nd 2ND LT. PEACHEY "C" Coy reported twice wounded on the 22nd	G.C

Army Form C. 2118.

WAR DIARY
or
INTELLIGENCE SUMMARY.
(Erase heading not required.)

Place	Date	Hour	Summary of Events and Information	Remarks and references to Appendices
BRIE	22/23 3.18		The Battn received orders to hold BRIE bridgehead, this order was cancelled, and the Battn was ordered to make forced march to hold bridge head and allow 24TH DIVISION to retire across the SOMME as the 61ST DIVN had fallen back, no one knew where, and it was thought the enemy might be found anywhere between the country, bounded by BRIE - MONS - ATHIES - MATIGNY - FALVY - ST. CRIE.	
	23.3.18		The Battn formed a defensive flank one which the DIVN fell back and the SOMME was crossed at FALVY on the afternoon of the 23rd. The whole Division fell back through the 8TH DIVN who occupied a line W of the SOMME. During the night of 23/24 the 20th M.G. Battn concentrated at LIHONS. 2ND LIEUT. F.J. MILLER 'B' Co reported wounded 2ND LIEUT H.W. FELLS "A" Co reported wounded	
LIHONS	23.3.18 24.3.18 25.4.18		In the early morning of the 25th the Battn was ordered to occupy the line HALLU - PUNCHY - HYENCOURT - LE - PETIT as it was ascertained that the 8th DIVN in front of us was broken, and the 24th had to fill in the gap, as the retirement progressed	US.B

Army Form C. 2118.

WAR DIARY
or
INTELLIGENCE SUMMARY.
(Erase heading not required.)

Instructions regarding War Diaries and Intelligence Summaries are contained in F. S. Regs., Part II. and the Staff Manual respectively. Title pages will be prepared in manuscript.

Place	Date	Hour	Summary of Events and Information	Remarks and references to Appendices
PUZEAU	25.3.18		The Battn moved to a front of Infantry in FOUCHETTE - PUZEAU - ONICOURT line at about 1.30 p.m. In position by 3 p.m., withdrew from Infantry line about midnight. Infantry advanced about 10 a.m. to co-operate with the French attack at 11 a.m. were pushed back. Guns occupied previous nights positions. About 8 a.m Infantry withdrew on CHAULNES followed by guns. In position N. & S. of CHAULNES Station by 6 p.m. Quiet night. Broke shelled nunned position with 5.9's. about 8.15 to 8.45 am no Infantry action	
	26.3.18		At about 10 a.m. it was discovered the Infantry of the DIVISION, who 1st ROYAL FUSILIERS with whom the Battn H.Q. was, had been ordered to retire more than an hour previously. No order was given to the Battn at all. They remained in position and covered the retirement of the 1st ROYAL FUSILIERS	

WAR DIARY
INTELLIGENCE SUMMARY

Place	Date	Hour	Summary of Events and Information	Remarks and references to Appendices
	26.3.18		who had received no orders to withdraw, owing to a mistake. Finally on withdrawal and still without any orders, the Battn. concentrated with all available guns, at about 3 p.m. at ROSERES and took up a line with the Infantry of the Divn on line VRELY - ROUVROY, which was held until and during the nights 27/28. ROUVROY position abandoned, and line readjusted to run through WARVILLERS	
WARVILLERS	28.3.18		Enemy aft. heavy bombardment, attacked along whole of Divisional front, and to N. and S. at about 10.30 a.m. Attack in front of WARVILLERS completely held up, but troops on N & S. gave back; necessitated withdrawal from this village to avoid being cut off. Withdrawal carried out with difficulty and line taken up LEQUESNE-LE-CRIX and held until nearly 5 p.m. when a General withdrawal took place through BEAUMONT ENSANTERRE & VILLERS-AU-ERABLES, where Divn. concentrated at about 7 p.m. and moved by night, marching across country to CASTEL, and into Bivouacs at about 2 a.m. 29th inst. in BOIS DE SENEGAT	G.S.
BOIS DE SENEGAT	28/29			

Army Form C. 2118.

WAR DIARY
or
INTELLIGENCE SUMMARY.
(Erase heading not required.)

Instructions regarding War Diaries and Intelligence Summaries are contained in F. S. Regs., Part II. and the Staff Manual respectively. Title pages will be prepared in manuscript.

Place	Date	Hour	Summary of Events and Information	Remarks and references to Appendices
	29.3.18		Three Companies (8 Guns) attached to 17TH 72ND & 73RD BDES covering crossing of Stream at CASTEL. BN H.Q moved from BOIS DE SENECAT to (wood above HAILLES) and on to HAILLES CHATEAU COMPANIES IN POSITIONS AS FOLLOWS:— "A" Coy. Billets in HAILLES. "B" " - - - "C" " in position E of THEZY GLIMONT with 73RD I.B. "D" " in position N of "C" Coy with Infantry of 72ND I.B.	
	29/30			
	31.3.18		Dispositions as above except that "A" Coy occupied positions on E edge of wood above HAILLES.	
	1.4.18		"A" Coy positions moved to ridge above HAILLES Cemetery	
THEZY GLIMONT	2.4.18		"A" Coy withdrawn into Billets at THEZY	G.S.O
	5.4.18 4.4.18		Battn and 4 Coy's of 8 guns each, billeted in a state of preparedness for AA work in THEZY GLIMONT, 2nd Coy having 2 guns in action. Battn. Remained here until 4 a.m. 4.4.18 when they moved to the B. in BOIS DE. GENTELLES.	

Army Form C. 2118.

WAR DIARY
or
INTELLIGENCE SUMMARY.
(Erase heading not required.)

Place	Date	Hour	Summary of Events and Information	Remarks and references to Appendices
BOIS-DE-CENTELLES	4.4.18	Noon	A & D Coys. occupying positions from T.29.b in front of CENTELLES to S.W. corner of BOIS RELABE. B & C Coys in reserve. (MAP. 62d 1-100,000)	
		6 p.m.	B Coy moved to front occupied by 72nd BDE from 0.27.a. to left flank of "A" Coy.	
		11 p.m.	2 guns of "C" Coy sent to a position in 0.32.c. central to help to fill gap created by Infy. These positions were maintained, until Battn. was relieved. Guns of the 61st Divn. holding positions in 24th Divn. line, placed under command of 24th M.G. Battn. given afternoon of 4th April until relief, when they remained in the line with the 58th Divn.	
SALEUX.	6.4.18		Battn. relieved by the 58th M.G. Battn and entrained at SALEUX about 8 p.m.	
ST. VALERY.	7.4.18		The 24th Battn. M.G.C. detrained at ST. VALERY SUR SOMME on the night of the 6/7 April and marched to the 3RD ARMY REST CAMP W. of ST. VALERY. The following officers reported from the M.G.C. Base Depôt, and are posted to Companies as under :-	
			2ND LIEUT. TURBERVILLE H.C. "A" Coy.	
			" " TIDY F.	
			" " ROLLES H.D.	

Army Form C. 2118.

WAR DIARY
or
INTELLIGENCE SUMMARY.
(Erase heading not required.)

Place	Date	Hour	Summary of Events and Information	Remarks and references to Appendices
ST. VALERY	7.4.18			
	8.4.18		253 O.R's reported from M.G.C. Also reported Lieut. J.L.D. Buxton R.A.M.C. posted to this Battn. Officers reported to Companies as under:-	

"B" Coy.   2ND LIEUT. WILLIAMS F.C.
                     "   WALPOLE W.F.
                     "   BAINES F.
                     "   WESTHEAD G.

"C" Coy.   "   MASON L.A.
                     "   HUNT. E.J.K.
                     "   HOGGAN S.R.

HEADQUARTERS
2ND IN COMMAND   CAPT. J.B.GAWTHORPE
ADJUTANT.   2ND LT. H.H. ROBINSON.
INTELLIGENCE OFFICER.   2ND LT. W.E. BRIDGEMAN

"A" COMPANY
COMMANDING.   LIEUT. M.M. TIBBETT.
2ND IN COMMAND   LIEUT. C.G.G. GILBERT.

"B" COMPANY   LIEUT. E.M. RUNTZ.

Army Form C. 2118.

WAR DIARY
or
INTELLIGENCE SUMMARY.
(Erase heading not required.)

Instructions regarding War Diaries and Intelligence Summaries are contained in F. S. Regs., Part II and the Staff Manual respectively. Title pages will be prepared in manuscript.

Place	Date	Hour	Summary of Events and Information	Remarks and references to Appendices
ST. VALERY.	8.4.18		"C" COMPANY. COMMANDING. LIEUT. L. ANDERSON M.C. 2ND IN COMMAND LIEUT. G.W.A. WOOD. "D" COMPANY COMMANDING. CAPT. B. GREEN. 2ND IN COMMAND LIEUT. G.D. JAMES.	
SALLENELLE	9.4.18		C & D. Companies moved into Billets in SALLENELLE.	
	10.4.18		Battn H.Q.'s established in SALLENELLE	
	11.4.18		CAPT. J.B. GAWTHORPE is appointed 2ND in Command of the BATTN. 7.4.18.	
	13.4.18		LIEUT. BROWN rejoined from 17th INFY BDE.	
	16.4.18		A & B. Companies and Brunsport moved from 3RD ARMY REST CAMP, ST. VALERY and entrained at WOINCOURT and FRESSENNEVILLE respectively. 38 other Ranks joined the BATTN from M.G.C. Base Depot.	
	17.4.18		C & D Companies and H.Q's moved from SALLENELLE and entrained on the night of the 17/18th as follows:— "C" COMPANY. AT. WOINCOURT "D" COY & H.Q'S AT FRESSENNEVILLE	

Army Form C. 2118.

WAR DIARY
or
INTELLIGENCE SUMMARY
(Erase heading not required.)

Place	Date	Hour	Summary of Events and Information	Remarks and references to Appendices
BELVAL	18.4.18		A & C Coys detrained at PERNES and marched to Billets in CONTEVILLE and TROISVAUX respectively. D & B Coys detrained at BRYAS and marched to Billets in BETHONVAL and L'ABBAYE-DE-NEUVILLE FARM respectively. H.Q's detrained at BRYAS and marched to BELVAL where they remained in Billets for night.	
CONTEVILLE	19.4.18		H.Q's moved to CONTEVILLE. Disposition of Battalion on the 19.4.18. H.Q's & "A" Company — CONTEVILLE "B" Company — L'ABBAYE-DE-NEUVILLE FARM "C" " — TROISVAUX "D" " — BETHONVAL 18 other Ranks comprising No 5 SIGNALLING SECTION of DIVISIONAL SIGNALLING Coy., joined the Battn.	G.i.B

WAR DIARY
or
INTELLIGENCE SUMMARY.

Army Form C. 2118.

Place	Date	Hour	Summary of Events and Information	Remarks and references to Appendices
	20.4.18		The following Officers are Struck off the Strength of the Battn. 2ND LIEUT. JENKINS M.C. found unfit by MEDICAL BOARD, and returned to ENGLAND. 2ND LIEUT J.C. HOPWOOD to C.C.S. 30.3.18 2ND LIEUT. A.H. DOUGLAS to C.C.S. 1.4.18 TRAINING Companies parading under their own arrangements, carried out as much firing as possible, in order to ensure that Gun numbers get accustomed to their Guns, and all able to remedy quickly, Stoppages which commonly occur when in Action. 5 O.R's admitted to Hospital	W.S.B.
BELVAL.	21.4.18		"B" Coy. moved from L'ABBAYE-DE-NEUVILLE FARM to Billets in	

Army Form C. 2118.

WAR DIARY
or
INTELLIGENCE SUMMARY.
(Erase heading not required.)

Place	Date	Hour	Summary of Events and Information	Remarks and references to Appendices
CONTEVILLE	21.4.18		**TRAINING.** The greater part of the training now in progress, consists of the tactical handling of M.G. teams by Section Officers. As far as possible this work is made competitive, the object being to encourage the men to take a more enthusiastic interest in work, which before, in the elementary training was made irksome and boring. 1 O.R. was taken on strength as transfer from 2nd Battn M.G.C. and posted to "D" Coy. 1 O.R. admitted to Hospital.	16.B.
	22.4.18		**TRAINING.** Company Commanders carried out a Syllabus of Training including range work, and all points of Elementary M.G. training. N.C.O's paraded for Drill under the R.S.M. Range takers instructed on the Range Finder by the ARMOURER SERGEANT.	

WAR DIARY
or
INTELLIGENCE SUMMARY.

Army Form C. 2118.

Place	Date	Hour	Summary of Events and Information	Remarks and references to Appendices
CONTEVILLE	22-4-18		The Commanding Officer, Lieut. Col. N.I. Whitty D.S.O. delivered a lecture on Military Law at "B" Cor' H.Q. Belval, to all officers who had not previously Sat twice at a Courtmartial, as member of the Court.	U.S.B.
			2 O.R's admitted to Hospital	
	23-4-18		TRAINING	
			Lectures delivered to Section Officers, and the men of their Companies on the uses of AA Sights. Direct, Indirect and vertical fire. Practical demonstrations of the packing of limbers were also given, and afterwards carried out as a detail.	
			6 O.R's admitted to hospital.	

Army Form C. 2118.

WAR DIARY
or
INTELLIGENCE SUMMARY.
(Erase heading not required.)

Place	Date	Hour	Summary of Events and Information	Remarks and references to Appendices
CONTEVILLE	24.4.18		TRAINING. Coys. paraded under their own arrangements, to carry out the syllabus of training. The officers of each Coy were detailed to make a defence scheme for the Village, in which they were Billeted, submitting a sketch plan, showing dispositions of Guns allotted for the purpose. Major Gawthorpe gave a resume of Village defence scheme by Section officers.	
	25.4.18		Permission was given from the 24TH DIVN (A 90 261) for the following officers to wear the badges of the following ranks pending appearance of promotion in the LONDON GAZETTE. CAPT D. GREEN MAJOR LIEUT. L. ANDERSON M.C. MAJOR " E.M. RUNTZ MAJOR " E.M. TIBBETT CAPTAIN	V.S.B.

Army Form C. 2118.

WAR DIARY
or
INTELLIGENCE SUMMARY.
(Erase heading not required.)

Instructions regarding War Diaries and Intelligence Summaries are contained in F. S. Regs., Part II. and the Staff Manual respectively. Title pages will be prepared in manuscript.

Place	Date	Hour	Summary of Events and Information	Remarks and references to Appendices
CONTEVILLE	25.4.18		LIEUT. C.G.GILBERT CAPTAIN	
			" G.W.H. WOOD CAPTAIN	
			" G.D. JAMES CAPTAIN	
			" F. MORRIS CAPTAIN	
			2ND LIEUT. H.H. ROBINSON CAPTAIN	
			7 O.R's admitted to Hospital	
			MAJOR GAWTHORPE delivered a lecture to "C" Coy on General Principles of Machine Gun tactics.	16.6.
			TRAINING.	
	26.4.18		Company Commanders arranged their own programmes of training, to consist daily of One hour's mechanical work, 2 hour's Tactical work including firing on various natural ranges, ½ hour P.T. and ½ hour lecture.	
			50 O.R's joined the Batt'n from the BASE DEPÔT, and taken on the strength and posted to Companies	

Army Form C. 2118.

WAR DIARY
or
INTELLIGENCE SUMMARY.
(Erase heading not required.)

Instructions regarding War Diaries and Intelligence Summaries are contained in F. S. Regs., Part II. and the Staff Manual respectively. Title pages will be prepared in manuscript.

Place	Date	Hour	Summary of Events and Information	Remarks and references to Appendices
CONTEVILLE	26.4.18		Major Gawthorpe delivered a lecture to "D" Coy on improved methods of laying, and control for Barrage fire. Captain Gilbert & 2nd Lieut. Turberville ("A" Coy) attended on 73rd BDE tactical exercise.	
	27.4.18		The commanding officer Lieut. Col. N.I. Whitty D.S.O. inspected "A" Coy and transport at CONTEVILLE	
	28.4.18		The commanding officer Lieut. Col. N.I. Whitty D.S.O. inspected "D" Coy and Drums&fort at BETHONVAL 2nd Lieut. Williams T. reported to this Battn for Duty as Signalling Officer	

WAR DIARY or INTELLIGENCE SUMMARY.

Army Form C. 2118.

Place	Date	Hour	Summary of Events and Information	Remarks and references to Appendices
CONTEVIL-E	29.4.18		The usual Syllabus of training, including Range work, carried out during the morning. The C.O. Lieut. Col. N.I. WHITTY D.S.O. inspected "C" Coy and Transport in the morning and "B" Coy in the afternoon. 4 O.R's evacuated to C.C.S. and Struck of strength 2 O.R's admitted to Hospital Battn received orders from the DIVN. to prepare to move	I.S.B.
	30.4.18		"A" & "B" Coys leave CONTEVILLE at 5pm and proceeded to Billets in HOUDAIN. 4 O.R's transferred from the Battn to join 1st Battn M.G.C. 1 O.R's reported to the Battn and attached to H.Q's	

To: H.Q. 24th Divsn "G".

CONFIDENTIAL

WAR DIARY

OF

24th BATTn M.G.C.

From: 1.5.18.   To: 31.5.18.

(VOLUME 2).

MGC

for Bridgeman Lt.
for Lt. Col Commanding, 24th Battn M.G.C.

2.6.18.

Army Form C. 2118.

WAR DIARY
or
INTELLIGENCE SUMMARY.
(Erase heading not required.)

Instructions regarding War Diaries and Intelligence Summaries are contained in F. S. Regs., Part II. and the Staff Manual respectively. Title pages will be prepared in manuscript.

Place	Date	Hour	Summary of Events and Information	Remarks and references to Appendices
	1.5.18		H.Q's moved from CONTEVILLE to Billets for the night in DIVION.	
			C & D Coys moved from TROISVAUX and BETHONVAL respectively to Billets for the night in DIVION.	
			ROUTE OF MARCH VIA HUCLIER, VALHOUN, DIEVAL, OURTON.	
			A & B Coys marched to Billets in huts for the night in the BOIS DE NEULETTE	
LES BREBIS	2.5.18		A & B Coys moved from BOIS DE NEULETTE and relieved the Coys of the 3RD Div Canadian M.G. Battn in the line Loos. Taking our positions in the Left Brigade Sector of the Divisional Front.	
			C & D Coys moved from DIVION to occupy Billets vacated by A & B Coys in the BOIS DE NEULETTE	
			H.Q's moved from DIVION to Billets in LES BREBIS for the night.	
"	3.5.18		C & D Coys moved from the BOIS DE NEULETTE to Billets to complete the relief of the 3rd Canadian M.G. Battn in the Right Brigade Sector of the Divisional Front.	1&B

Army Form C. 2118.

WAR DIARY
or
INTELLIGENCE SUMMARY.
(Erase heading not required.)

Place	Date	Hour	Summary of Events and Information	Remarks and references to Appendices
LES BREBIS	3.5.18		H.Q's TRANSPORT & DETAILS Billets established in FOSSE II LES BREBIS	
"	4.5.18		Line now occupied by the 24th Div. M.G. Battn. Very quiet day, excepting for slight intermittent shelling. Little Enemy aerial activity. At about 11 p.m. Orders received from Division to prepare for an Enemy attack. Information received from prisoners, that the attack would be launched on a front extending from ROBECQ to LENS. 3 O.R's joined the Battn. today from Base Depôt. 4 O.R's Struck off the strength and evacuated Sick. 1 O.R. to 1st Army School.	
	5.5.18		Nothing unusual happened during the night. Early morning excepting slight retaliation for our harassing fire. Programme of work including P.T. Gas drill, Gun drill and Methods of Indirect Fire under Details Officer	

Army Form C. 2118.

WAR DIARY
or
INTELLIGENCE SUMMARY.
(Erase heading not required.)

Place	Date	Hour	Summary of Events and Information	Remarks and references to Appendices
LES BREBIS	5.5.18		Special instruction to N.C.O's under P.T & Gas N.C.O's 2 O.R's admitted to Hospital. The following Officers reported to the Battn for Duty from Base Depôt 4.5.18 and posted to the Coys as shewn:- Lieut. G. Logan "A" Coy. 2nd " A. M. Cooke "D" " 2nd " H. Todd "D" "	
"	6.5.18		Information received from Bosche prisoners that attack will be launched on our front at 10.30 pm night 9/10. Concentration of German Tanks reported to be in FOURNES & WAVRIN. Watch Officer in charge of the Guns in Divisional Reserve reconnoitred positions in FOSSE 7 to be manned in case of attack developing from the N.	

Army Form C. 2118.

WAR DIARY
or
INTELLIGENCE SUMMARY.
(Erase heading not required.)

Place	Date	Hour	Summary of Events and Information	Remarks and references to Appendices
LES BREBIS	6.5.18		Enemy particularly quiet during the day with slight increasing Artillery activity in our forward areas during the night	
"	7.5.18		Very quiet day, increased harassing fire by our Artillery towards evening. Enemy retaliation very slight, excepting few shells in the afternoon in the BARLIN NOEUX LES MINES area.	
"	8.5.18		Inter-Company reliefs arranged, whereby the O.C. Coy or 2nd in Command, and at least one other officer per Coy, and one Senior N.C.O. & 1 Composite Gun Team are at Details Camp H.Q's. Hostile operations practically NIL, our harassing fire still maintained, especially on ENEMY back areas & likely concentration points. Our Aircraft very active throughout the day. 2ND Lieut. H.C. Holmes evacuated from F.A. to Hospital and Struck off the strength accordingly. 1 O.R. admitted to Hospital.	K.S.B.

Army Form C. 2118.

WAR DIARY
or
INTELLIGENCE SUMMARY.
(Erase heading not required.)

Place	Date	Hour	Summary of Events and Information	Remarks and references to Appendices
LES BREBIS.	9.5.18		Special preparations and orders issued for action in case of probable attack, to-night. Enemy preparation from a reconnaissance by our own flying aeroplanes, indicates the Enemy's intention to attack at an early date. Enemy Artillery quiet. Our Harassing fire increased. One Battalion of Tanks moved past H.Q's to position on the LENS BETHUNE ROAD, under cover of a Smoke barrage from our batteries in rear. 1 O.R. returned from Hospital and taken on strength of H.Q Coy. 1 O.R. admitted to F.A. 1 O.R. rejoined Corps Gas School.	45.F.

Army Form C. 2118.

WAR DIARY
or
INTELLIGENCE SUMMARY.
(Erase heading not required.)

Place	Date	Hour	Summary of Events and Information	Remarks and references to Appendices
LES BREBIS	10.5.18		All quiet on Div Front during the night. Nothing unusual happened. Enemy retaliated during the day on our forward trench system with various calibre shells. Enemy Aeroplanes more active, flying at medium height over our Trench system, but not crossing them. Weather fine & bright but visibility not good. 3 O.R's admitted to F.H.	
"	11.5.18		Enemy artillery more active during the day. Slight shelling (single calibre) in the vicinity of FOSSE II. Our M.G's fired 17,000 rounds:- Harassing fire on Cross Roads and Dumps behind the Enemy's lines. Enemy Aircraft flying low over the trenches yesterday, one brought down by M.G fire. 1 O.R wounded from hospital. 1 O.R returned from leave 1 O.R admitted to hospital	As B

Army Form C. 2118.

WAR DIARY
or
INTELLIGENCE SUMMARY.
(Erase heading not required.)

Instructions regarding War Diaries and Intelligence Summaries are contained in F. S. Regs., Part II. and the Staff Manual respectively. Title pages will be prepared in manuscript.

Place	Date	Hour	Summary of Events and Information	Remarks and references to Appendices
LES BREBIS	12.5.18		Quiet night excepting a slight Shelling of FOSSE II with small calibre shells. Our Artillery carried out the usual harassing fire programme. Our M.G's fired 15,000 rounds on suspected M.G. emplacements, Cross Roads, Tracks and Dumps. One M.G claims to have silenced an Enemy machine gun last night.	
LES BREBIS	13.5.18		Quiet night. LES BREBIS heavily shelled at about 7.30 and again at 11 pm. Quiet night. Rather more than per usual intermittent shelling of our forward areas in the morning. Enemy Balloons up in the evening. No Aerial activity, and little shelling on either side. Enemy Shelled the Areas between LOOS and MAROC during the morning and early afternoon. 2 small calibre shells fell in the vicinity of FOSSE II near BATTN. H.Q's 5 O.R's Reported from Base Depot taken on strength and posted to Coys	6.5.B

Army Form C. 2118.

WAR DIARY
or
INTELLIGENCE SUMMARY.
(Erase heading not required.)

Instructions regarding War Diaries and Intelligence Summaries are contained in F. S. Regs., Part II. and the Staff Manual respectively. Title pages will be prepared in manuscript.

Place	Date	Hour	Summary of Events and Information	Remarks and references to Appendices
LES BREBIS	14.5.18		Much quieter along whole front, becoming active at night time, when enemy shelled gun positions in front of HILL 70.	
			Major DODD. S.C.F. attached 24th Batt. M.G.C. proceeded on leave to U.K.	
	15.5.18		4. O.R's evacuated to C.C.S. and struck off strength	
			1. O.R. reported for duty.	
			Enemy more active against back areas, also increased activity against our trench system. All gun positions report increased shelling in their vicinity	
			1. O.R. admitted to F.A.	
			1. O.R returned from Leave.	
	16.5.18		Rather active in the afternoon. Left Coy H.Q. shelled heavily for about 4 hours with 250 5.9 shells — no casualties.	
			6. O.R. reported from BASE DEPÔT as Signallers.	
			3. O.R. reported from Hospital.	
			Lieut C. L. DEWHIRST admitted to Hospital.	
	17.5.18		Activity fairly normal. Three gun positions report shelling in their vicinity Enemy M.G's a little more active towards midnight	K.i.F.
			2nd Lieut W. M. McINTYRE admitted to Hospital.	

Army Form C. 2118.

WAR DIARY
or
INTELLIGENCE SUMMARY.
(Erase heading not required.)

Instructions regarding War Diaries and Intelligence Summaries are contained in F. S. Regs., Part II. and the Staff Manual respectively. Title pages will be prepared in manuscript.

Place	Date	Hour	Summary of Events and Information	Remarks and references to Appendices
LES BREBIS	18.5.18		Enemy artillery very active in the LOOS area all day. Front line also received attention.	
			Our artillery very active the whole day and night.	
			2nd Lieut. G.W. PETRIE proceeded to attend a course of instruction at CORPS SCHOOL.	
			3. O.R. admitted to Hospital.	
	19.5.18		Much more activity than usual - probably retaliation for our strafe of yesterday. The front line shelled heavily, also LOOS, and eastern edge of ST PIERRE.	
			2nd Lieut. M.W.T BROWN reported from Hospital	
			3. O.R reported for duty with this Battn.	
			3. O.R reported for duty from Hospital	
			At 7 a.m. we successfully co-operated in a raid made by the Right Brigade of the 11th DIVISION on our left. We fired a barrage, using 6 guns of the LEFT COMPANY. 22,000 rounds of S.A.A. were fired.	
	20.5.18		Fairly active throughout the day. Several of our gun positions shelled, probably in retaliation for our harassing fire of the previous night. LES BREBIS, and Mine in East of NOEUX-LES-MINES shelled in the evening. Captain G.P. MORRIS joined this Battalion from BASE DEPÔT, and assumed command of "A" Company. 1. O.R. died of wounds received yesterday	

(A8004) Wt W1771/M2031 750,000 5/17 **Sch. 82** Forms/C2118/14 D. D. & L., London, E.C.

Army Form C. 2118.

WAR DIARY
or
INTELLIGENCE SUMMARY.
(Erase heading not required.)

Instructions regarding War Diaries and Intelligence Summaries are contained in F. S. Regs., Part II. and the Staff Manual respectively. Title pages will be prepared in manuscript.

Place	Date	Hour	Summary of Events and Information	Remarks and references to Appendices
LES BREBIS	21.5.18		Very active in the morning. About 100 shells fell in the vicinity of LEFT COY. H.Q. 3 Gun positions report slight gas shelling in their vicinity aft mid-night. 5. O.R. admitted to Hospital 1. O.R. reported from Hospital.	
	22.5.18.		Increased gas shelling in the DIVISIONAL AREA. Enemy field guns active throughout the day against our out-posts, becoming normal towards mid-night.	
	23.5.18.		LOOS and MAISINGARBE shelled during the day. Enemy M.G.s show more activity against our M.G. positions. More activity against back areas in retaliation for our Artillery harassing fire. 3. O.R. admitted to Hospital, and struck off strength.	
	24.5.18.		Increased activity against our line in front of LOOS. Gun positions in the vicinity of LOOS CRASSIER report direct hits on the trenches. 2. O.R. admitted to F.A. 2. O.R. admitted to Hospital	

WAR DIARY
or
INTELLIGENCE SUMMARY

Army Form C. 2118.

Place	Date	Hour	Summary of Events and Information	Remarks and references to Appendices
LES BREBIS	25.5.18		LEFT BRIGADE H.Q. shelled at mid-day. Battery positions in LOOS shelled with 4.2's at mid-night. Normal activity on rest of DIVISIONAL FRONT. 2nd Lieut H.C. Holmes reported from BASE DEPOT from Hospital. 2.O.R. admitted to Hospital, and struck off strength.	
	26.5.18		Quiet day, increasing activity towards mid-night; nearly the whole of the BLUE LINE system receiving attention, and afterwards intermittent shelling of the RED LINE. No infantry action followed. During the night 26/27, the Battalion was re-arranged on a three-company front with one company in reserve. 2nd Lieut H.C. HOLMES admitted to Field Ambulance.	
	27.5.18		2.O.R. evacuated to C.C.S. and struck off strength accordingly. Enemy carried out harassing fire on our left front at irregular intervals, especially in the vicinity of LOOS, and HARRISON'S CRATER (Coy. H.Q.) The last named was shelled with 4.2's at 6 p.m. Activity below normal on the rest of the Divisional front. 4.O.R. wounded, and evacuated to C.C.S. 5.O.R. admitted to Hospital, and struck off strength accordingly.	

Army Form C. 2118.

WAR DIARY
or
INTELLIGENCE SUMMARY.
(Erase heading not required.)

Instructions regarding War Diaries and Intelligence Summaries are contained in F. S. Regs., Part II. and the Staff Manual respectively. Title pages will be prepared in manuscript.

Place	Date	Hour	Summary of Events and Information	Remarks and references to Appendices
LES BREBIS	28.5.18		Enemy gas-shelled several points during the day and night. Atmospheric conditions greatly favoured this. MAROC gas-shelled heavily from 12.30 a.m to 3 a.m, also CITÉ ST PIERRE at mid-day until 4 P.m. I.O.R. admitted to Fd Amb. I.O.R. returned from Hospital.	
	29.5.18		MAROC VILLAGE and CRASSIER heavily shelled with about 400 5.9's from 11.30 a.m to 1 P.m. LOOS also received attention from light field guns at 10.30 a.m. General activity during the night above normal. I.O.R. admitted to Fd Amb. I.O.R. returned from D.R.S.	
	30.5.18		Enemy artillery active against our left Brigade front from 2 p.m to 4 p.m LOOS trench also shelled at intervals during the day. Intermittent harassing fire with 4.2's of the DOUBLE CRASSIER and HARRISON'S CRATER (Centre Coy. H.Q) from 9-11 P.m. I.O.R. wounded, admitted to Hospital.	
	31.5.18		MAROC and S.E. of MAROC shelled heavily during the morning. Slight gas shelling in the vicinity of 3 Centre Coy gun positions between 9 and 11 P.m. E.A's fairly active, flying very high. Practically no retaliation for gas projected by us during the night. 1.O.R. reported, and taken on strength of this Battalion.	W.B

CONFIDENTIAL.

WAR DIARY

OF

24th Battn M.G.C.

From 1.6.18. To. 30.6.18.

(Volume 8).

Place	Date	Hour	Summary of Events and Information	Remarks and references to Appendices
				Reference attached map showing dispositions of 24th Battalion Machine Gun Corps.
LES BREBIS	1.6.18		Enemy activity quiet during day, increasing towards night time. MAROC shelled at 11 a.m. Slight gas shelling on CENTRE Coy GUNS at mid-night. RIGHT Coy AREA shelled heavily in the afternoon. 2nd LIEUT. W. L. MacINTYRE evacuated to base, and struck off strength accordingly. Situation Normal.	
	2.6.18.		The usual enemy activity against certain points. PREVITE CASTLE and LEFT Co Y. H.Q. shelled considerably with 4.2's during the morning. Slight gas shelling in vicinity of FOSSE Y during the night. Cross Roads in M.5. shelled during the night.	
	3.6.18		Very quiet day. Shelled church in MAROC during the night. 6. O.R's reported from BASE DEPOT, taken on strength, and posted to Companies. 2. O.R's rejoined from Hospital. The following extract from London Gazette Supplement dated 3rd June:— The King has been pleased, on the occasion of His Majesty's birthday to approve of the following reward for distinguished service in connection with Military Operations in FRANCE and FLANDERS:— Military Cross. Capt. B GREEN. Bucks Bn. Oxford & Bucks L.I. attd 24th Battn M.G.C.	

Army Form C. 2118.

WAR DIARY
or
INTELLIGENCE SUMMARY.
(Erase heading not required.)

Place	Date	Hour	Summary of Events and Information	Remarks and references to Appendices
LES BREBIS	4.6.18		With the exception of the usual shelling of LOOS with field guns, the day very quiet. Enemy bombarded LOOS-HULLUCH ROAD during the night.	
			1. O.R. rejoined from D.R.S.	
			1. O.R. wounded accidentally	
			1. O.R. admitted to F.A.	
	5.6.18		We successfully co-operated in a raid made by the 9th ROYAL SUSSEX last night. The LEFT COY fired a barrage of 6 guns, and the CENTRE COY co-operated with a barrage from 6 guns. 22,500 rounds of S.A.A. were fired. Enemy retaliated rather heavily about mid-night after the raid, and shelled FOSSE V, and gas-shelled the area round LEFT COY H Q AND PRENITE CASTLE	(S.6)
			1 O.R. rejoined from D R S	
			1 O.R. admitted to F.A.	
			1 O.R. rejoined from Hospital	
			Situation Normal. - Very quiet during the day, becoming active against our forward communications at dusk. Several of our gun positions report shelling in retaliation for our harassing fire.	
	6.6.18.		1. O.R. wounded admitted to F.A.	
			1. O.R. rejoined from BASE DEPOT, and taken on strength	

WAR DIARY or INTELLIGENCE SUMMARY.

Army Form C. 2118.

Place	Date	Hour	Summary of Events and Information	Remarks and references to Appendices
LES BREBIS.	7.6.18		Enemy showed a little more activity to-day. The usual harassing in the vicinity of LOOS. FOSSE v. shelled with 4.2s at 6 p.m. and a little later the LENS-BETHUNE ROAD - also at intervals during the night. LEFT COY. H.Q. established in BRIGADE. H.Q. - PREVITE CASTLE, vacated by the 73rd INFANTRY BRIGADE. 1. O.R. evacuated to C.C.S. and struck off strength. 1. O.R. admitted to HOSPITAL. B. Coy. in Reserve, relieved C. Coy (CENTRE COY) in the line on the night 7/8th. C. Coy. relieved B. guns of B. Coy. in reserve positions. Remaining guns and teams of C. Coy came into reserve at Batt. H.Q. FOSSE 11. (FOSSE 2.)	
	8.6.18.		Very quiet all day. A few salvoes of 4.2. on LENS-BETHUNE ROAD at intervals from 11p.m. to 3 a.m. 8/9th. LT. C.L. DEWHIRST returned from Hospital. 20. O.Rs. reported from BASE DEPÔT, and are taken on the strength of the Battalion.	
	9.6.18		Several of our CENTRE COY guns report retaliation for our nightly harassing fire. 2/LT. M.B. LOCKE returned from ANTI-GAS COURSE. 5. O.R's returned from Hospital.	

Army Form C. 2118.

WAR DIARY
or
INTELLIGENCE SUMMARY.

(Erase heading not required.)

Instructions regarding War Diaries and Intelligence Summaries are contained in F. S. Regs., Part II. and the Staff Manual respectively. Title pages will be prepared in manuscript.

Place	Date	Hour	Summary of Events and Information	Remarks and references to Appendices
LES BREBIS	10.6.18		Very quiet day. From 9 p.m. until midnight, the LENS-BETHUNE ROAD shelled intermittently with 4.2s. Slight gas-shelling in this area also. 1 O.R reported from BASE DEPÔT and taken on strength.	
	11.6.18		Quiet day. Normal activity until night-time when enemy steam unusually active. Many points on the Divisional front received attention. 2nd Lieut. A.S. LINLEY and 2nd Lieut. F.J. PHILLIPS reported from BASE DEPÔT and taken on strength of the Battn., and posted to "B" and "C" Coys. respectively.	
	12.6.18		Much more active to-day. LOOS shelled intermittently all day with 4.4 and 4.2s. Front and Support lines in vicinity of HILL 70 heavily shelled also. 1 O.R admitted to F.A.	
	13.6.18		Frequent gas shelling throughout the day on LOOS between 10 and 11 p.m. enemy at midnight on Reserve Coy H.Q. and LENS-BETHUNE ROAD. The following Officers of the Battn. awarded decorations as below:- MAJOR J. JOYCE M.C. — D.S.O. 2nd LIEUT. PEACHY A.N. — M.C. 2nd LIEUT. PETRIE C.W. — M.C. 2nd LIEUT. TRENT W.A. — M.C. 2nd LIEUT. HOPWOOD J.G. — M.C. 4 O.R's awarded the D.C.M. Special D.R.O. 3735 dated 13/6/18 The above are immediate awards for operations from the night 21st 3.18 to 25.3.18.	R.B

D. D. & L. London, E.C.

Army Form C. 2118.

WAR DIARY
or
INTELLIGENCE SUMMARY.
(Erase heading not required.)

Place	Date	Hour	Summary of Events and Information	Remarks and references to Appendices
LES BREBIS	14.6.18		Enemy activity normal. Slightly increased shelling of our forward system at night. 2ⁿᵈ LIEUT. T.R. FRANCIS reported from BASE DEPÔT, and posted to "C" COY. 7 O.R's. admitted to F.A.	
	15.6.18		CITÉ ST PIERRE shelled in the early afternoon, also other points on the RIGHT COY. FRONT - elsewhere fairly quiet. 15 O.R's. admitted to Hospital 1 O.R. reported from BASE DEPÔT, and taken on strength. Enemy shelled during the day in retaliation. Frequent shelling of our front line during the night. 21. O.R's. admitted to F.A.	
	16.6.18		There is a very prevalent form of sickness throughout the Division, resulting in a large decrease in strength of Battⁿ.	
	17.6.18		Very quiet during day - Intermittent gas shelling at night. 11. O.R's. admitted to F.A. LEFT COY co-operated in a successful raid made by the 13ᵗʰ MIDDLESEX at 6 p.m. 4 GUNS fired 4,200 rounds on selected targets	

Army Form C. 2118.

WAR DIARY
or
INTELLIGENCE SUMMARY.
(Erase heading not required.)

Place	Date	Hour	Summary of Events and Information	Remarks and references to Appendices
LES BREBIS	18.6.18		Enemy particularly quiet. Back areas have not been shelled during the past 48 hours, and very little shelling of our trench system reported. One of our planes brought down 9.30 a.m. near LOOS by E.M.G. fire was shelled by 4.2 during day. We supported a raid made by the 11th Sherwood Foresters of the Division on our left, the LEFT COY firing a barrage of 4 guns on HONEY ALLEY, and HULLUCH TRENCH 10,450 rounds of S.A.A. were fired. An abnormal number of Ambulances observed in the enemy lines during the past week. The probability is that the Boche is suffering from the same complaint as our own troops. 44 O.R's evacuated to C.C.S. and struck off strength accordingly.	
	19.6.18		Artillery on both sides was quiet during the day, but each side showed signs of activity at night-fall. Between 11 p.m. and 1 a.m. our artillery became active, probably covering the raid in progress on our right. Enemy artillery retaliated on batteries in CITÉ ST PIERRE. Our machine guns carried out harassing fire on the usual targets near work, centres of activity, and tracks. Enemy retaliation was weak. LOOS TRENCH, and light railway being traversed during the night. Bombs were dropped on LOOS during night. 29. O.R's admitted to F.A. 1. O.R injured from F.A	K.B.

Army Form C. 2118.

WAR DIARY
or
INTELLIGENCE SUMMARY.
(Erase heading not required.)

Instructions regarding War Diaries and Intelligence Summaries are contained in F. S. Regs., Part II. and the Staff Manual respectively. Title pages will be prepared in manuscript.

Place	Date	Hour	Summary of Events and Information	Remarks and references to Appendices
LES BREBIS	20.6.18		Quiet day. Naval intermittent shelling of various points. Dumps in LOOS, also light railway received attention from field guns, and machine guns at night. 16 O.R's admitted to F.A.	
	21.6.18		Very quiet day. A few shells only on St PIERRE, and the usual light shelling of LOOS. 20. O.R's. admitted to F.A.	
	22.6.18		Activity on both sides below normal.— becoming active towards night. Prisoners captured on 1st Army front make statements proving that the enemy is suffering from the prevailing disease. One Division was unable to relieve owing to it. 27. O.R's. admitted to F.A.	
	23.6.18		Fairly quiet day — our back areas shelled with long range H.V. guns in the evening and night. 2/Lt. W.F. WALPOLE admitted to F.A. 6. O.R's. admitted to F.A.	

WAR DIARY
or
INTELLIGENCE SUMMARY.

(Erase heading not required.)

Army Form C. 2118.

Place	Date	Hour	Summary of Events and Information	Remarks and references to Appendices
LES BREBIS	24.6.18		Left Coy. front shelled with light calibre, also several sweeping gas shells fell near CASINO gun positions. E.A's bombed Support line in M.12 26. O.R's admitted to Fd Amb. 4. O.R's reported from BASE DEPÔT and taken on strength	
	25.6.18		Renewed activity on dumps in LOOS at night time. Slight gas shelling of back areas towards night-time. Increased activity all round. 15. O.R's admitted to Fd Amb. Scots Alley and LOOS-HULLUCH ROAD shelled during the day with 4.2's. Also active on LEFT and RIGHT COY's front and back areas during the early evening. Lt. VICKERY returned from leave to U.K. 8. O.R's admitted to Fd. Amb.	
	26.6.18		At 8.a.m. this morning, we co-operated in a very successful raid on the enemy lines by the 1st ROYAL FUSILIERS, 4 guns of CENTRE COY., and 2 guns of RIGHT COY. firing a barrage. 16,000 rounds of S.A.A. were fired. We suffered no casualties, and the two prisoners captured afforded very valuable identification. They belonged to the 86th Res. Division which relieved the 220th Division during the night 21/22nd inst.	K.B.

WAR DIARY
or
INTELLIGENCE SUMMARY.

Army Form C. 2118.

Place	Date	Hour	Summary of Events and Information	Remarks and references to Appendices
LES BREBIS	27.6.18		Enemy more active than usual. Vicinity of HILL 70. shelled with 4.2s. FOSSE 12 shelled with gas shells, and RIGHT COY H.Q. shelled for 40 minutes, also GREEN POST and DUNHILL POSITIONS. 4 O.R's admitted to HOSPITAL	
	28.6.18		Quiet day. Front line shelled in the evening also HILL 70. CYCLONE gun shelled about mid-night. 11 O.R's rejoined from HOSPITAL. 29 O.R's returned from HOSPITAL.	
	29.6.18		Very much more active than usual especially towards dusk. Northern edge of LOOS shelled with 4.2's at 10.30 p.m. also HILL 70 at about this time. A generally increased activity all round. Enemy M.G's unusual activity.	
	30.6.18		2/LT. WALPOLE rejoined from HOSPITAL. 13 O.R's rejoined from HOSPITAL. A little less activity during the day, but very active at intervals during the night. The light railway in ST PIERRE shelled at 9.30 p.m. During the past fortnight, a noticeable increased activity against our communications, and light railways. It is evident that this new enemy division identified by the raiding party of the 1st FUSILIERS is endeavouring to make things much more lively on this front. 14 O.R's rejoined from HOSPITAL.	E.B.

24th BATTALION.
MACHINE GUN
CORPS.

Vol 5

CONFIDENTIAL

WAR DIARY.

OF

24th BATTN M.G.C.

From. 1.7.18.   To.   31. 7. 18.

(VOLUME 4.)

Army Form C. 2118.

WAR DIARY
or
INTELLIGENCE SUMMARY.
(Erase heading not required.)

Instructions regarding War Diaries and Intelligence Summaries are contained in F. S. Regs., Part II. and the Staff Manual respectively. Title pages will be prepared in manuscript.

Place	Date	Hour	Summary of Events and Information	Remarks and references to Appendices
LES BREBIS	1.7.18		Quiet day. A noticeable increased activity from enemy M.G.s at night time. Enemy appears to be doing work under direct fire. 25. O.R.s rejoined from hospital.	
	2.7.18		Very quiet during the day. Enemy Heavy artillery active again against our back areas at night. Reports show an increased activity from hostile heavy shelling during the night. 28. O.R.s rejoined from hospital. 10. O.R.s admitted to hospital.	
	3.7.18		A very noticeable increased activity from our own aircraft. Enemy trench mortars & night light guns & trench mortars active. First trench mortar shell hill 70 receiving particular attention. 13. O.R.s rejoined from hospital. 2. O.R.s admitted to hospital.	
	4.7.18		Lewis gun postings report hostility in their vicinity also much activity against our light railways & forward communications at dusk. Enemy Trench mortars & Light trench mortars active at 10 p.m until 12.m. As before, activity followed. 19. O.R.s rejoined from hospital. 8. O.R.s admitted to hospital.	A.P.

WAR DIARY or INTELLIGENCE SUMMARY

Army Form C. 2118.

(Erase heading not required.)

Place	Date	Hour	Summary of Events and Information	Remarks and references to Appendices
LES BREBIS.	5.7.18		With the exception of slightly increased enemy aerial activity, the day was very quiet. Uneventful. Our A.A. guns kept up heavy + several occasions succeeded in preventing the E.A's from crossing our lines. 7. O.R's rejoined from hospital. 8. O.R's admitted hospital.	
	6.7.18		Quiet day. I.M.S's retaliated vigorously for an hour's fire about the night.	
	7.7.18		Quiet day. Enemy seemed active at dusk — continual activity against our trenches. Free grass especially on the night. group.	
	8.7.18		5. O.R's rejoined from hospital. Very quiet day, with the exception of usual intermittent harassing fire and enemy retaliation for our continued harassing fire every night.	
	9.7.18		9. O.R's rejoined from hospital. Enemy appear to be very jumpy, sending up enormous quantities of very lights. During the twilight + standing up many aerial lights E.A.'s very active on the enemy. An E.A. brought down by us of our planes at about 9 p.m. 2 O.R's admitted hospital. 3 O.R's rejoined from hospital.	
	10.7.18		Very quiet day. Used 100 flying ops. E.A's seen in front of letter Brebis during. 81 O.R's rejoined from hospital.	

WAR DIARY or INTELLIGENCE SUMMARY

Army Form C. 2118.

Place	Date	Hour	Summary of Events and Information	Remarks and references to Appendices
LES BREBIS	11.7.18		Fairly quiet day excepting shelling of Mazingarbe from 7 p.m. until 8.30 p.m. Much artillery activity. Much directed against our M.G. posts. 1 O.R. injured from hostile.	
	12.7.18		Gt co-operated in a raid made by the 8th Queens on Bruay line at 8.30 a.m. Centre & Right pups each firing a minute from 4 guns. Most of the enemy activity directed against an abnormal amount takes place between 10 p.m. & 2 a.m. So otherwise no unusual activity. 4 O.R's reported from Base Depot as re-inforcements were taken on strength of this Battn.	
	13.7.18		3 O.R's rejoined from hospital. Left Coy H.Q & Reserve Posts bombed, shelled during the early afternoon. Enemy his incessantly interrupted G. Sector. Several gun positions in night bombing. A few were hit by their patrols. Enemy to be established report shelling. Intensive fire. 1 O.R. rejoined from hospital.	
	14.7.18		Very light bombardment of Cité St Pierre from 5 p.m. until 12 midnight. Most of the shells fell in the vicinity of OPERA HOUSE & OSLER SQUARE.	

Army Form C. 2118.

WAR DIARY
or
INTELLIGENCE SUMMARY.
(Erase heading not required.)

Instructions regarding War Diaries and Intelligence Summaries are contained in F. S. Regs., Part II. and the Staff Manual respectively. Title pages will be prepared in manuscript.

Place	Date	Hour	Summary of Events and Information	Remarks and references to Appendices
LES BREBIS.	15.7.18		Enemy showed signs of increasing activity – shelling MAROC, St. PIERRE & lately the Cite d'formed system and des FOSSES 7 again. The dull weather prevented any aircraft operations. 2 O.R's new pavements from trade depot, & taken on strength of Battn. 1. O.R. admitted to hospital.	
	16.7.18		Enemy shelling directed more against areas S. of the LENS BETHUNE RD. MAROC. ST PIERRE & FOSSEY. Fair amount of retaliation. shrapnel arms to the front installation. 4 O.R's rejoined from hospital 1 O.R. admitted to hospital.	
	17.7.18		Several salvoes of H.E. Shrapnel, on the front posts – otherwise quiet. Our artillery very active especially against enemy trench areas at night time. 13 O.R's rejoined from hospital.	
	18.7.18		Increased shelling of the whole system also the H.E. increase in gas shelling, at daylight time. After a very quiet day, enemy put down a heavy barrage, at 10 p.m. extending to BLUE LINE lasting for about 1 hour & 15 mins. 3 O.R's admitted to hospital. 1 O.R. rejoined from hospital.	
	19.7.18		Very quiet day, opening up the usual harassing in and [...] with Z.A.M. Enemy appears to have a very strong signals to Sie of Colonels Lt US 40 O.R's new draft on strength of [...] reported Base Depot and taken on strength of the Battalion [...] 2 O.R's admitted to hospital	

Army Form C. 2118.

WAR DIARY
or
INTELLIGENCE SUMMARY
(Erase heading not required.)

Place	Date	Hour	Summary of Events and Information	Remarks and references to Appendices
LES BREBIS	20/7/16.		Enemy placed increased retaliation for our nightly harassing fire. In some cases replying to find out of this our batteries. ROLLES. A.D. A Coy. presented sick to ENGLAND & others. Strength.	
	21/7/16.		1 O.R. reported from hospital. LOOS, & the LOOS-LENS RD received more attention than usual during the night.	
	22/7/16.		About 185 gas shells in LOOS during the day. In co-operation in a raid made by the 7th NORTHAMPTONSHIRE RGT. on enemy Cavel system in vicinity of HUNT SAP. at 2 p.m. Left group firing a barrage from 5 guns + Centre group co-operating with a barrage from 6 guns. 11 O.R's reported from Brit Depot & Everson strength of the Batt.	
	23/7/16.			
	28/7/18.		Enemy rather more active during the early evening, shelling the LOOS-LENS RD & LOOS, while 10. P.M. ABT The LOOS CRASSIER received attention during the evening. 2. O.R's wounded — Much M/s strength.	
	24/7/16.		Own battery in Reply brought shells heavily from now 15. 4 p.m. and again at midnight. ABT The LOOS 1 O.R. reported from hospital. 1.O.R. admitted to hospital.	1(c)

WAR DIARY or INTELLIGENCE SUMMARY

Army Form C. 2118.

Place	Date	Hour	Summary of Events and Information	Remarks and references to Appendices
LES BREBIS	25.7.18		Very quiet day. E.A. went heavy fire at night. E.A. dropped 4 bombs in BRACQUEMONT and an O.R. admitted to E.A. at 9 p.m. at FOSSE 10. 2.O.R.s rejoined from hospital. 3. O.R.s struck off strength.	
	26.7.18		LOOS shelled intermittently with 5.9's between 8.30 + 9.30 p.m. Enemy H.V.'s shelled in back areas between them.	
	27.7.18	2 p.m.	2.O.R. admitted to hospital + struck off strength. Enemy artillery very active at night, replying vigorously to our harassing fire. E.A.'s active over our back system during early morning + in the evening.	
	28.7.18		Right group area shelled during the afternoon. St PIERRE OPERA HOUSE, + Group H.Q in OSKER SQUARE LOOS shelled throughout the night at intervals. 2.O.R's admitted to hospital.	A/1
	29.7.18		Enemy artillery very active, again shelling to house point 94 gas shells fell into LOOS at 10 p.m. to 11 p.m. Wind dispersed gas rapidly and no casualties down to night. 2 O.R's admitted to hospital.	

Army Form C. 2118.

WAR DIARY
or
INTELLIGENCE SUMMARY.
(Erase heading not required.)

Place	Date	Hour	Summary of Events and Information	Remarks and references to Appendices
LES BREBIS.	30.7.18.	p.m.	LENS BETHUNE RD shelled from 9.30. to 11.30 p.m. at intervals. E.A's has shown a marked increase in activity. One E.A over N.I. dropped two bombs and some tiny bombs dropped in C.R. St PIERRE. 1.O.R reported from Base Depot & taken on strength. 2.O.R.'s admitted to hospital. Enemy particularly quiet during the afternoon. Slight shelling in the vicinity of O.G.1. HARTS & HARRISON'S CRATERS from 9.30 to 10 a.m.	89.6
	31.7.18.		1.O.R. admitted to hospital (Gastric) & 1.O.R. reported from Base Dept.	

CONFIDENTIAL

WAR DIARY.

OF

4th Battn M.G.C.

From. 1.8.18. to 31.8.18.

VOLUME 6.

Army Form C. 2118.

WAR DIARY
or
INTELLIGENCE SUMMARY.
(Erase heading not required.)

Instructions regarding War Diaries and Intelligence Summaries are contained in F. S. Regs., Part II. and the Staff Manual respectively. Title pages will be prepared in manuscript.

Place	Date	Hour	Summary of Events and Information	Remarks and references to Appendices
LES BREBIS	1-8-18		Enemy showing increased activity. - Shelling St. PIERRE, MAROC and LOOS. E. Aeroplanes very busy bombing our back areas during the night.	
	2-8-18		2. O.R.s rejoined from the Base. Enemy heavy artillery shelling our back areas during the day. Intermittent shelling of the whole front area - especially O.G.1 and OPERA HOUSE St. PIERRE. 1. O.R. admitted to hospital.	
	3-8-18		Been quiet both day & night - indifferent weather prevented any aircraft operations. Lieuts W.J. LANGSTAFFE & C.B.E. Gilbert proceeded to M.B.C. guns course at L.H.Q. School. 2nd Lieut WALPOLE proceeded to Corps Gas School for course. 1. O.R. admitted to hospital.	S.D.B.

Army Form C. 2118.

WAR DIARY
or
INTELLIGENCE SUMMARY.
(Erase heading not required.)

Instructions regarding War Diaries and Intelligence Summaries are contained in F. S. Regs., Part II. and the Staff Manual respectively. Title pages will be prepared in manuscript.

Place	Date	Hour	Summary of Events and Information	Remarks and references to Appendices
LES BREBIS.	4-8-18.		Enemy fairly active against our forward crews, causing also some shelling of LIEVIN & HULLUCH RD. - Mostly Shrapnel. 3. O.R.s rejoined from hospital.	
	5-8-18.		The G.O.C. 24th Div. Maj. Gen. Daly, C.B. inspected H.Q. & transport of the Battalion. Increased gas shelling of several points including E. 30. central & vicinity of our positions E. of St PIERRE. Enemy showed unusual activity during the night. Major R. Brew , & Capt. T. Morris rejoined from course of instruction. 4. O.R.s admitted to hospital.	LSB
	6-8-18.		Normal activity on both sides - Intermittent shelling (gas) in several points including FOSSE 12. 2. O.R.s admitted to hospital.	

Army Form C. 2118.

WAR DIARY
or
INTELLIGENCE SUMMARY.
(Erase heading not required.)

Place	Date	Hour	Summary of Events and Information	Remarks and references to Appendices
LES BREBIS.	7.8.18		Enemy firing action against LOOS vicinity of OPERA HOUSE. Jr PIERRE - Shelling with 5.9's for 4 hrs. Lots flying enemy aeroplanes active during the morning over LOOS CRASSIER. I.O.R rejoined the Battalion from hospital.	
	8.8.18		Enemy seems to concentrate all attention on the night prep of Distrinal Front. especially area in and around St. PIERRE. I.O.R. admitted to hospital.	
	9.8.18		Exceptionally quiet day. A few salvoes of shells on night prep area at midnight. Bad weather prevented air reconnaissance. 2. O. R's reported from Base Depôt & taken on the strength of the Battalion.	L.a.B.

Army Form C. 2118.

WAR DIARY
or
INTELLIGENCE SUMMARY.
(Erase heading not required.)

Place	Date	Hour	Summary of Events and Information	Remarks and references to Appendices
LES BREBIS.	10.8.18		Faulty action by enemy on general areas – killing the usual party including FOSSE 16. LES BREBIS shelled with H.V. in the evening. 2 O.R.s admitted to hospital.	
	11.8.18		Heavy calibre shells fell into OSTEN Sq this morning near Bn H.Q. Enemies artillery seem to be quieter at night especially on roads in LOOS. 2/Lieut WALPOLE rejoined from attd 91st Bde at Corps Ptn School.	
	12.8.18		3 O.R.s admitted to hospital. On retaliation for the enemy's incessant shelling has been very severe and especially to-day shew in bombard his immediate area with all calibre shells several times during the day. 1 O.R. killed in action.	L.B.

WAR DIARY
or
INTELLIGENCE SUMMARY

Army Form C. 2118.

Place	Date	Hour	Summary of Events and Information	Remarks and references to Appendices
LES BREBIS	13.8.18		The area between LOOS & MAROC received most attention from the enemy especially during the night. 1. O.R. rejoined from hospital.	
	14.8.18.		Enemy shelled our area very lively during the morning, most of this shelling was directed against the mines in and about NOEUX LES MINES. FOSSE 10 also shelled during the afternoon. LOST Gas Shell during the night. 1. O.R. wounded & 2. O.R. admitted to hospital.	
	15.8.18.		Much hostile gas shell area last night - PETIT SAINS, BRAQUEMONT, HAZINGARGHE, & FOSSE 10 were treated several times - causing several casualties. Enemy artillery quieter than usual excepting slight hostile gas shelling in the vicinity of LOOS. 3. O.R.s admitted to hospital.	

Army Form C. 2118.

WAR DIARY
or
INTELLIGENCE SUMMARY.
(Erase heading not required.)

Place	Date	Hour	Summary of Events and Information	Remarks and references to Appendices
LES BREBIS	Aug 1918. 16.		Enemy apparently very nervous – sending up many Very lights during the night & a harassing bombardment at odd times in our front area.	
	17.		Enemy M.G's show little activity & practically no retaliation for our incessant harassing fire. Capt. B.B.A. Lord proceeded on course of instruction at Army Infantry School. Continuous activity against Hole front especially the vicinity of DOUBLE CRASSIER, LOOS & ST PIERRE. 6. O.R's admitted to hospital. 1. O.R. rejoined from hospital.	
	18.		Very quiet during the day. At 8.30 p.m. enemy shelled LOOS & HULLUCH RD with gas shells but the effect was extremely owing to the very high wind. 2nd Lieut G.H.C. Turnbull admitted to hospital. 2. O.R.'s admitted to hospital.	W.O.B.

WAR DIARY
or
INTELLIGENCE SUMMARY.
(Erase heading not required.)

Army Form C. 2118.

Place	Date	Hour	Summary of Events and Information	Remarks and references to Appendices
LES BREBIS	Aug 19.		Very quiet excepting rather heavy shelling of FOSSE V. MAROC. Child killed by 4 hrs. 1.O.R. admitted to hospital.	
	20.		LOOS + ST PIERRE again shelled heavily after a comparatively quiet day, shelling of the latter place for 15 mins. Gas. Men letters Bdier Croisier & Major Shelled Lewley during the morning. Major Ruutz proceeded to attend a course at Army Musketry Camp. 1.O.R. rejoined from Base.	
	21.		Quiet during the day becoming rather furious when shelled LOOS at intervals during the night + FOSSE 14 with gas shells at 10 P.m. Lieut Dewhurst proceeded to England for 6 months to instruct at home.	
	22.		In co-operation with a raid on the enemy trenches made by the 8th Batt. The Rifle Brigade at 4.45 a.m. The raid was found [W.A.B.] to be unoccupied and no enemy were encountered	W.A.B

Army Form C. 2118.

WAR DIARY
or
INTELLIGENCE SUMMARY

(Erase heading not required.)

Instructions regarding War Diaries and Intelligence Summaries are contained in F.S. Regs., Part II. and the Staff Manual respectively. Title pages will be prepared in manuscript.

Place	Date 1918	Hour	Summary of Events and Information	Remarks and references to Appendices
LES BREBIS	Aug. 23		Increasing activity against our back areas and battery positions. Enemy shells were freely during the bombardments. LENS-BETHUNE Rd shelled at odd intervals.	
	24		Capt Tillott proceeded on Coy Commander's Course at Divisional Reception Camp. Lieut W.L. Long s/s/r admitted to hospital. FOSSE 5 shelled in the evening and at 7.15 p.m. enemy put down a pretty heavy barrage on our front line N.of LOOS. 2nd Lieut Rice returned from leave to U.K. 2nd Lieut Todd proceeded to Corps Gas School for Course Gas schools. 2nd Lieut Rodgers proceeded to England for 14 days leave.	
	25		Quiet during day. Shelled on both sides towards evening, LOOS + trenches E. of LOOS shelled with gas shells at intervals during the night. 1. O.R. rejoined from hospital. 3. O.R.'s admitted to hospital	16/5

(1030) Wt W3509/P715 750,000 3/18 E 2688 Forms C/2118/16.

Army Form C. 2118.

WAR DIARY
or
INTELLIGENCE SUMMARY.
(Erase heading not required.)

Instructions regarding War Diaries and Intelligence Summaries are contained in F. S. Regs., Part II. and the Staff Manual respectively. Title pages will be prepared in manuscript.

Place	Date 1918	Hour	Summary of Events and Information	Remarks and references to Appendices
LES BREBIS	Aug. 26		MAROC, LOOS TOWER BRIDGE, & the LENS — BETHUNE RD. shelled heavily at dusk & between 10 & 11 p.m. — otherwise normal activity during the day. 2 O.R.s admitted to hospital. 1 O.R. rejoined from hospital.	
	27.		Several batches of heavy shells, probably 8", fell into LIEVIN during the morning. Taken over the left Bgde front of 20th Div on our right — La Fosse. The 22nd Div being on the right side of 15th Div — the left group guns & forming night group with H.Q. in ANGRES. Left Brigade relieved by left group guns were now run & form night group with H.Q. in ANGRES. 2nd Lieut C.F. Bartlett to Englebelmer hospital & others off strength. Gun action at intervals and attacks generally normal.	W.O.
	28		CITÉ DES GARENNES gas shelled during the greater part of the night. 5 O.R.s rejoined from Base. 3 O.R.s admitted to hospital.	

(1930. Wt. W5300/P713. 750/000 3/18 E 2688 Forms C/2118/16.)

Army Form C. 2118.

WAR DIARY
or
INTELLIGENCE SUMMARY.
(Erase heading not required.)

Place	Date 1918	Hour	Summary of Events and Information	Remarks and references to Appendices
LES BREBIS	Aug. 29		Back area again receiving considerable attention from enemy long range + H.V. guns. Forward Communication + MAIN ST. ST. PIERRE shelled heavily at odd times during the night. There has been a noticeable increase in amount of shelling of centre group area during the past 3 days. Lieuts A.C.M. DYMOCK + M.J. ELFICK reported from M.S.C. Base Dept. and taken on strength – also 2nd Lieut F.S. FAIT. 1 O.R. admitted to hospital.	L.B.
	30.		Quiet during daytime. Fairly heavy shelling of Centre group H.Q. vicinity. S.R. co-operated in a raid on the enemy trenches made by the NORTH STAFFS at 12.30 – 29/30 inst. 1 O.R. wounded (gas shell). 1 O.R. admitted to hospital.	
	31.		HARTS CRATER + vicinity shelled with gas shells – also ferried system shelled during the night. Enemy aeroplanes over positions in front during the early morning.	

CONFIDENTIAL

WAR   DIARY.

of

24th BATTALION MACHINE GUN CORPS.

From 1/9/18   to   30/9/18.

(Volume   6)

Army Form C. 2118.

WAR DIARY
or
INTELLIGENCE-SUMMARY.
(Erase heading not required.)

Instructions regarding War Diaries and Intelligence Summaries are contained in F. S. Regs., Part II and the Staff Manual respectively. Title pages will be prepared in manuscript.

Place	Date	Hour	Summary of Events and Information	Remarks and references to Appendices
FOSSE 41 (LES BREBIS)	1/9/18		Situation normal.	
		2O-15p.m.	The vicinity of M.G. 13, and POODLE Gun positions in the right group was shelled.	
		10-30	Centre Company reports that bombs were dropped on CITE ST PIERRE near enough to their Headquarters for the concussion to be felt.	
			1 O.R. was wounded and struck off strength, & 1 O.R. admitted to Hospital.	
	2/9/18	11-0p.m.	2nd Lieut H.Todd rejoined from Course at Corps Gas School.	
			Bombs were again dropped on ST PIERRE in the vicinity of the Centre Group Head Quarters.	
			2 O.R. were admitted to Hospital, & 1 O.R. returned from Hospital.	
			Capt. G.D.James proceeded on Company Commanders Course at Divisional Reception Camp.	
			Major B.Green proceeded on leave to PARIS.	
	3/9/18.		During the day, the Vally in front of POODLE position was shelled.	
			Lieut. Col. Whitty D.S.O. proceeded to G.H.Q. M.G.School (Special Course).	
			Major J.B.Gawthorpe assumed command,having returned from Paris leave on this day.	
			2 O.R. struck off strength having been in F.A. more than 7 days. 1 O.R. admitted to Hospital.	
			& 1 O.R. admitted to Base Hospital and struck off strength.	
	4/9/18		GREEN CRASSIER was shelled during the morning. No damage was done to M.G. positions though infantry posts were temporarily evacuated.	
			3 O.R. admitted to Hospital.	
			1 O.R. reported from Base Hospital.	
	5/9/18.	00-30	Gas Masks were worn in the vicinity of N 29d 20.70. when enemy shelled, using Mustard Gas.	
		2 p.m.	77,500 rounds of S.A.A. were expended during the week on Harrasing fire.	
			Major I.Anderson M.C. proceeded on leave to U.K. and 2nd Lieut Picker assumed command of "C" Company.	
	6/9/18.	10pm & 11"	Lieut. Langstaff W.L. was evacuated to England, and struck off strength accordingly.	
			2 O.R. were admitted to Hospital.	
			The vicinity of M.G. 19 was shelled with gas shells.	
			2 O.R. were admitted to Hospital.	
	7/9/18.		Situation normal.	
			2 O.R. rejoined from Hospital, and 2 O.R. were admitted to Hospital.	
	8/9/18.		"B" Coy in the line was relieved by "A" Coy in reserve at FOSSE 2.	
			The relief took place by day, and gun kit was carried on pack animals. "B" came into Billets at FOSSE 2. "A" Coy is now on the right sector.	
			1 O.R. admitted to Hospital (gassed)	
			2 O.R. " " "	

Army Form C. 2118.

WAR DIARY
or
INTELLIGENCE SUMMARY.
(Erase heading not required.)

Instructions regarding War Diaries and Intelligence
Summaries are contained in F.S. Regs., Part II.
and the Staff Manual respectively. Title pages
will be prepared in manuscript.

Place	Date	Hour	Summary of Events and Information	Remarks and references to Appendices
	8/9/18		1 O.R. rejoined from Hospital.	
	9/9/18		Major J.S.Harper joined the Battalion as 2nd I/C, and assumed command; Major J.B.Gawthorpe proceeding to England prior to going to America, Major Gawthorpe is therefore struck off strength. 2nd Lieuts Laughland, and Knott, to be Lieuts. 1 O.R. to Hospital.	
	10/9/18.		1 O.R. reported from Base. Small shells fell near BARLING BRUNFITT, and M.G.19 positions. Capt G.D.James returned from Company Commanders Course. 1 O.R. admitted to Hospital.	
	11/9/18.		Lieut Col Whitty resumed command on return from Course. 1 O.R. taken on strength from hospital. 2 O.R. to Hospital. 2 O.R. from Hospital. 1 O.R. wounded (slightly) and is struck off strength.	
	12/9/18		2nd Lieut. Rodgers returned from leave to U.K. 2 O.R. rejoined from Hospital. 4 O.R. struck off strength having been in F.A. more than 7 days. Lieut. G.Logan proceeded to Divisional Reception Camp for Company Commanders Course. 69,000 rounds of S.A.A. were expended on harrasing fire during the week.	
	13/9/18.		The trench, and entrance to the dug-out at R 11 position were blown in by 5-9'shell, about 30 fell in the vicinity. Lieut. P.W.Brown proceeded on a musketry course. Major B.Green returned from French leave. Major E.M.Runtz returned from Musketry Course. 2nd Lieut. W.H.Stringer reported for duty to this Unit from the Base. 1 O.R. reported from Base.	
	14/9/18.		Capt G.D.James proceeded on leave to U.K. 1 O.R. admitted to Hospital.	
	15/9/18.		Back areas were shelled including FOSSE 2 during the day. G.O.C. Division attended Church Parade at FOSSE 2. 2 O.R. rejoined from Hospital. 4 O.R. admitted to hospital.	
	16/9/18.		The situation still remains normal. 1 O.R. evacuated to C.C.S. and struck off strength. 3 O.R. evacuated to C.C.B.	
	17/9/18.		1 O.R. to hospital, 1 O.R. to hospital, 2 O.R. struck off strength, having been in F.A. over 7 days.	

WAR DIARY or INTELLIGENCE-SUMMARY.

Army Form C. 2118.

(Erase heading not required.)

Instructions regarding War Diaries and Intelligence Summaries are contained in F. S. Regs., Part II. and the Staff Manual respectively. Title pages will be prepared in manuscript.

Place	Date	Hour	Summary of Events and Information	Remarks and references to Appendices
	18/9/18	7-30pm	The night firing position at M.30b.92.48 was shelled, and 2 direct hits were received on the emplacement.	
	19/9/18.		2nd Lieut Bridgeman took over from Capt Robinson as Adjutant, while Capt Robinson is on leave. 2 O.R. were evacuated to C.C.S. and struck off strength. 1 O.R. rejoined from Hospital. 121,550 rounds of S.A.A. were expended on harrassing fire during the week.	
	20/9/18.		"C" Coy in the Line (Right Sector) was relieved by B Coy (in reserve at FOSSE2). The relief took place by day, excepting the GREEN CRASSIER guns, which were relieved night of 19/20. Gun Kit was carried on Pack animals.	
	21/9/18.		Capt H.H.Robinson proceeded on leave to U.K. Lieut C.G.Gilbert returned from leave(U.K.) his leave having been extended to 19/9/18. 3 O.R. were admitted to Hospital.	
	22/9/18.		BRUIFITT position was shelled throughout the day, and received 3 direct hits, 2 O.R. being wounded, 1 remaining at duty, and 1 admitted to Hospital, and struck off strength. Lieut C.G.Gilbert transferred from A to B Coy as 2nd i/c, A/Capt F.Norris transferred from B to A Coy. 1 O.R. to Hospital. 1 O.R. from Hospital. 5 O.R. evacuated to C.C.S. and struck off strength. Lieut H.J.Harris proceeded to course at M.G.H.Q.	
	23/9/18.		This morning re-organisation of Right Group was started. Capt Wood returned from Army Infantry course. Major I.Anderson rejoined from leave U.K. 2 O.R. admitted to Hospital. 2nd Lieut.H.Picker proceeded to Coy Commanders' Course at Divisional Reception Camp.	
	24/9/18.		The neighborhood of R.11 position was harrassed by M.G. fire at night. Lieut. Logan took over from 2nd Lieut Bridgeman as acting Adjutant.	
	25/9/18.		Completion of move of guns of right group notified. They are as follows :- SOUTH POINT N. GINGER BULLY SOUTH POINT S. PICKLE MACONACHIE CONSTANCE CHUTNEY PORK PRUDENCE BEANS Positions shewn on attached map. 1 O.R. evacuated and struck off strength. 3 O.R. from Hospital.	Map attached

Army Form C. 2118.

WAR DIARY
or
INTELLIGENCE-SUMMARY.
(Erase heading not required.)

Instructions regarding War Diaries and Intelligence Summaries are contained in F. S. Regs., Part II. and the Staff Manual respectively. Title pages will be prepared in manuscript.

Place	Date	Hour	Summary of Events and Information	Remarks and references to Appendices
	26/9/18.		In support of operations farther South, this Division made a demonstration in which 21 guns of this Battalion took part. Zero hour was 5-5 am. Programme was as follows :- Z-2+30 Bombardment by trenchmortars and 6" How's. 2+30, 17th Inf Brigade put up dummy figures 2+1 intense fire by Machine Guns and 18 Pdrs, 2+1 daylight, normal harrassing fire. Enemy retaliation was feeble. Machine Guns fired 54,700 rounds. 2 O.R. admitted to Hospital. 68,200 rounds of S.A.A. were expended on harrassing fire during the week.	
	27/9/18. 12mn to 2 am		A number of 4.2's fell near SUN & MOON positions. 1 O.R. to Hospital. 11 O.R.s from Base Depot, 3 O.R.s from Hospital (1 rejoined) 1 O.R. to Hospital.	
MAISNILLES RUITZ.	28/9/18.		Relief by the 58th Battalion which was to have taken place on the 28th, has been postponed 24 hours. Officers of the 58th arrived to reconnoitre prior to taking over this sector.	
	29/9/18		The 24th Battalion in the line in the Lens Sector was relieved by the 58th, and on relief proceeded to MAISNILLES RUITZ by Bus. The relief of all positions (less GREEN CRASSIER) was conducted by day.	
		2-0 pm	24th Battn Transport left FOSSE 2.	
		4-0 pm	"C" Coy (in reserve) and H.Q.Coy left FOSSE 2 by Bus.	
		10-0 pm	"A" Coy & "B" Coy less 2 sections arrived at MAISNILLES RUITZ.	
		1-15am	1 section "B" Coy and "D" Coy arrived. GREEN CRASSIER guns were late in arriving owing to their having to be relieved by night. Lieut. H.D.Buxton proceeded on leave to U.K.	
MAISNILLES		7-30am	Battn left here.	
		9-50am	Battn arrived at HERSIN to entrain for BOUQUEMAISON via ST POL at 9-45 am.	
		12-50am	Train left HERSIN.	
		6-00pm	Arrived BOUQUEMAISON.	
		9-00am	Transport left MAISNIL LES RUITZ to take its place in the Divisional Column at 11-15 am to proceed by march to PERNIN and thence to rejoin Battalion in the training area.	
BOUQUEMAISON COULLEMONTS	30/9/18	6-0pm 8-15pm	The Battalion detrained here. Having marched from BOUQUEMAISON, this village was reached at this hour, and Head Quarters were established here. A & B Coy's are also billetted in the village. C & D being in HUMBERCOURT, the neighbouring village. The billets are very dirty and bad.	

CONFIDENTIAL.

WAR DIARY

OF

24TH BATTN. M.G.C.

From 1.10.'18 To 31.10.'18

(Volume 7)

WAR DIARY
or
INTELLIGENCE SUMMARY.
(Erase heading not required.)

Army Form C. 2118.

Place	Date	Hour	Summary of Events and Information	Remarks and references to Appendices
COULLEMONT	1st	11.40 a.m.	Battalion billeted in Training Area. H.Q. A. and B. Coy at COULLEMONT C & D Coy at HUMBERCOURT. Transport arrived having spent the night in the neighbourhood of PENIN	
	2nd		All Companies carried out training	
	3rd		Ditto	
	4th		Advanced parties left to prepare new area which is in old French zone and quite demarcated.	
	5th	11.15 a.m.	Transport of A Coy and B. echelon of the transport left by road for new area. Battalion sports in the afternoon.	
	6th		Battalion entrained at MONDICOURT under Brigade arrangements.	
LOCK 6 CANAL DU NORD	7th	09.00	By 09.00 hrs Battalion concentrated in bivouacs close to LOCK 6. CANAL DU NORD having marched from detraining stations. During morning companies were allotted to Brigades as follows:— H.Q and B and C. Coys — 72nd Inf Bde. A. Coy — 14th Inf Bde D. Coy — 93rd Inf Bde	

Army Form C. 2118.

WAR DIARY
or
INTELLIGENCE SUMMARY.
(Erase heading not required.)

Place	Date	Hour	Summary of Events and Information	Remarks and references to Appendices
LOCK 6. CANAL DU NORD (cont.)	7th (cont.)		During afternoon, H.Q. and all Companies moved to areas occupied by Brigades concerned, and by dark were disposed of as follows:—	
WEST OF CANTAING			H.Q. and B. and C. Companies in trenches just WEST of CANTAING. A and D Coys - In trenches and bivouacs along ANNEUX—CANTAING ROAD.	
WEST OF RUMILLY.	8th	06.00	63rd DIVISION attacked at 04:30 and at 06.00 hrs 72nd Inf. Bde. with Bn H.Q. and 'B' and 'C' Coys. moved to supporting position about 1000 yards W. of RUMILLY. During morning, A and D Coys moved forward with their affiliated Brigades to positions vacated by 'B' and 'C' Coys. During afternoon and evening, B and C Coys relieved the guns of the 63rd Dvn. on a front N and just E. of NIERGNIES. Enemy attacked at NIERGNIES during relief, and drove in advanced posts, but did not retake village. Direct hits by 5.9 shells on a section of 'C' Coy as they were unlimbering from limbers, did great damage to gun equipment and killing 5, and wounding 8. O.R. By dawn relief complete, and battalion disposed in positions for attack at dawn as follows:—	
	9th		"B" Coy echeloned on left flank covering slopes into CAMBRAI, with one section forward to follow closely leading infantry, and assist consolidation.	

Army Form C. 2118.

WAR DIARY
or
INTELLIGENCE SUMMARY.
(Erase heading not required.)

Instructions regarding War Diaries and Intelligence Summaries are contained in F. S. Regs., Part II. and the Staff Manual respectively. Title pages will be prepared in manuscript.

Place	Date	Hour	Summary of Events and Information	Remarks and references to Appendices
W. of RUMILLY.	9th contd.		"C" Coy echeloned on right with one section forward to follow leading infantry, and assist in consolidation.	
		01.30	About 01.30.hrs. "D" Coy were ordered to take up barrage positions in trench just W. of N.W. end of NIERGNIES, to put down barrage 1st just S.W. of and 2nd just N.E. of AWOINGT. This company had great difficulty in finding their exact position in the dark, and only got their last gun correctly laid 30 seconds before ZERO, which was at 05.00 hrs.	
		05.00	At ZERO, under a very heavy artillery and M.G. Barrage, the infantry advanced, 9th EAST SURREY REGT on LEFT and 8th ROYAL WEST KENT REGT on right. Very little resistance was met with, the enemy having retired, except for a few men.	
		08.00	By 8 A.M. all objectives were gained, and the M.G.s were established in positions as under:— "B" Coy.— 1 section on ridge N. of AWOINGT. 3 sections on high ground between AWOINGT and NIERGNIES. "C" Coy.— 1 section on high ground 500 yds S. of AWOINGT. 3 sections about NIERGNIES CEMETRY.	

Army Form C. 2118.

WAR DIARY
or
INTELLIGENCE—SUMMARY.
(Erase heading not required.)

Instructions regarding War Diaries and Intelligence Summaries are contained in F.S. Regs., Part II. and the Staff Manual respectively. Title pages will be prepared in manuscript.

Place	Date	Hour	Summary of Events and Information	Remarks and references to Appendices
N of RUMILLY	9th		During the morning, the 73rd Inf. Bde continued the advance passing through the 72nd Inf. Bde. "A" Coy accompanied the 73rd Inf. Bde and by dusk the infantry and M.G.s were established on a line E and N.E. of CAUROIR, the enemy still holding CAGNONCLES with a few M.G.s At dusk, the battalion was disposed as follows:— H.Q. in AWOINGT A Coy in forward position supporting 73rd Inf. Bde B } Concentrated about 500 yds N. of NIERGNIES C } D in NIERGNIES 2/Lt BURY. F.H. reported from BASE DEPOT, is taken on strength, and posted to "D" Company	
AWOINGT	10th	03.00	At about 03.00 hrs 8 guns of "D" Coy moved up to behind ridge 1500 yds S.E. CAUROIR position ready to cover by direct fire infantry advance at dawn. Remaining 8 guns "D" Coy moved after dawn to just N. of main CAMBRAI—LE CATEAU ROAD. N. of AWOINGT At dawn the 73rd Inf. Bde advanced without opposition, the enemy having retired.	

Army Form C. 2118.

WAR DIARY
or
INTELLIGENCE SUMMARY.
(Erase heading not required).

Place	Date	Hour	Summary of Events and Information	Remarks and references to Appendices
AWOINGT.	10th		During the morning the advance was continued, "D" Coy moving forward with the Infantry, followed by "A" Coy, "B" Coy accompanying the 42nd Inf Bde, and "C" Coy with the 73rd Inf Bde.	
		1200	By about 12.00 hrs. RIEUX and AVESNES. LES. AUBERT had been occupied, and the enemy located holding ST AUBERT, and the high ground N. of AVESNES.	
			During the afternoon, the 13TH MIDDLESEX REGT supported by 8 guns D Coy attempted to seize high ground N. of AVESNES, but were unsuccessful.	
			At dark, the battalion was disposed as follows:—	
			H.Q. – RIEUX TOWER.	
			"A" Coy – RIEUX TOWER	
			"B" – CAUROIR.	
			"C" – RIEUX.	
			"D" – 4 guns on railway SOUTH of AVESNES.	
			4 guns near the bridge N.W. of RIEUX on NAVES-SAULZOIR ROAD.	
			8 guns in RIEUX.	
			The enemy used a great deal of gas shell throughout the afternoon, and evening rendering movement often difficult	
RIEUX TOWER.	11th	05.00	At about 05.00 hrs. the 14th Inf Bde passed through the 73rd Inf Bde, with the intention of taking ST AUBERT, and the high ground N of AVESNES, but the enemy resistance	K.R.D.

Army Form C. 2118.

WAR DIARY
or
INTELLIGENCE SUMMARY.

(Erase heading not required.)

Instructions regarding War Diaries and Intelligence Summaries are contained in F.S. Regs., Part II. and the Staff Manual respectively. Title pages will be prepared in manuscript.

Place	Date	Hour	Summary of Events and Information	Remarks and references to Appendices
RIEUX TOWER	11th		resistance proved so stiff that this could not be done. 8 guns of "D" Coy which were to move forward and consolidate the high ground, when gained, were only able to reach the slopes 1000 yds. N.E. of RIEUX, where they dug in, under M.G. fire, suffering heavy casualties, 2/Lt. J.A. RICE being killed, and 2/Lt. M.W.T. BROWN wounded. This position was maintained till dusk, when the 8 guns withdrew to RIEUX.	
		10.00	About 10.00 8 guns of "C" Coy moved through ST. HILAIRE to fire on S.E. side of ST. AUBERT, but the failure of the Infantry to advance made this unnecessary, and the guns returned to AVESNES.	
		11.00	About 11.00 8 guns of "B" Coy took up position in railway cutting just N.E. of AVESNES STATION, and fired on E. slopes of high ground. These guns were forced to withdraw on the failure of the Infantry attack. By dark, the Battalion was disposed as follows:-	
OUTSKIRTS OF AVESNES.			H.Q. with 17th Inf. Bde on S.W. Outskirts of AVESNES. "A" Coy - RIEUX TOWER. "B" - High ground S. of AVESNES "C" - In position on E, N.E, and N outskirts of AVESNES. "D" - RIEUX.	

Army Form C. 2118.

WAR DIARY
or
INTELLIGENCE SUMMARY.
(Erase heading not required.)

Instructions regarding War Diaries and Intelligence Summaries are contained in F.S. Regs., Part II. and the Staff Manual respectively. Title pages will be prepared in manuscript.

Place	Date	Hour	Summary of Events and Information	Remarks and references to Appendices
AVESNES.	12		Aeroplanes and patrols report that no enemy are in ST AUBERT or W. of LA SELLE RIVER. Patrols were pushed forward and advance continued on yesterdays frontage.	
		09:00	Battn. H.Qrs. moved at 09:00 to West outskirts of ST AUBERT. new those of 17th Inf. Bde.	
W. outskirts of ST AUBERT.			The Bttn. is holding EAST side of LA SELLE RIVER. 'A' Coy. moved forward to billets in ST AUBERT. 'B' " is forward on left. 'C' " is forward and has 4 guns in V.16.b. Central 'D' " is in reserve at RIEUX.	
		18.20	At 18:20 the QUEENS aided by M.G. and artillery barrage, crossed the river but were unable to stay there.	
	13.		Situation remains unchanged, the enemy being too strong to move by local attack. 'D' Coy. moved up to ST AUBERT — billets bombed at night — 1 O.R. killed. 'A' Coy. relieve 'B' Coy. who move to billets in VILLERS-EN-CAUCHIES.	
			New barrage positions sited by 'D' Coy on forward slopes. 'A' Coy still remaining in line. 4 M.G.s of 'A' Coy moved to positions in V.16.b.67. 4. M.G.s at V.16.b.00. and 8 M.G.s at V.9.b.15.	
	14th		These fired on repeated calls by Infantry to cover them in HAUSSY. 'B' Coy in billets in VILLERS. EN. CAUCHIES. 'C' Coy in billets in ST AUBERT. 2. Sections of 'D' Coy. went forward to dig emplacements N.W. of HAUSSY	155 B

Army Form C. 2118.

WAR DIARY
or
INTELLIGENCE SUMMARY.
(Erase heading not required.)

Place	Date	Hour	Summary of Events and Information	Remarks and references to Appendices
ST AUBERT	15th		'A' Coy were relieved by 'B' and 'C' Coys, and then moved to billets vacated by 'B' Coy in VILLERS-EN-CAUCHIES. 'B' Coy ordered to co-operate in operation by the 72nd Inf Bde. to establish a bridge-head E. of River. 8 guns to go forward with the Infantry, and 8 guns to find a barrage from the WEST side of the river. No 5 SECTION under 2/Lt STRINGER is to accompany 1st Battn NORTH STAFFS and No 6 SECTION under 2/Lt A. LINLEY to 8TH BATTN. ROYAL WEST KENTS, the remaining two sections relieving 'A' Coy in battery positions in V.9.a.5.5.	
		16.00.	'B' Coy H.Q. moved to V.9.a.8.4. During the night 'C' Coy relieved 8 guns of 'A' Coy and 8 guns went to positions on ridge overlooking HAUSSY. MAJOR B. GREEN. M.G. O.C. 'D' Coy - wounded.	
	16th		During the night 15/16 No 5 Section of B Coy were heavily shelled on the way to assembly positions, and being finally reduced to 1 OFFR. and 3 O.R's could not go forward. The NORTH STAFFS. also did not reach their assembly positions. As soon as the Infantry had reached their objectives, a sub-section of No 6 section under 2/Lt A. LINLEY crossed the river, and took up positions on the railway embankment at V.4.d.6.9. The attack was launched at 05.30.	

Army Form C. 2118.

WAR DIARY
or
INTELLIGENCE SUMMARY.
(Erase heading not required.)

Instructions regarding War Diaries and Intelligence Summaries are contained in F.S. Regs., Part II. and the Staff Manual respectively. Title pages will be prepared in manuscript.

Place	Date	Hour	Summary of Events and Information	Remarks and references to Appendices
ST AUBERT.	16th	02.00	"D" Coy moved up at 02.00 to positions in V.16.a.5.4. to fire barrage for assault of HAUSSY.	
		05.40	These guns remained in position to time required by S.O.S.	
		05.30	The attack was launched at 05.30 hrs and at about 09.00 news was brought that all objectives had been gained, excepting those on the left, which the NORTH STAFFS failed to reach, and about 400 prisoners and several machine guns were reported taken. (This report was confirmed later.)	
		09.00	No definite news was to hand regarding the left flank, but the line now ran from the railway crossing in V.4.d.6.9. through the SAND PIT, thence along sunken road to junction of road in V.11.b.35.55, to road junction in V.12.a.05.95 along EAST outskirts of HAUSSY to CEMETRY, thence due WEST to River. At this time, the 9th EAST SURREYS were mopping up the remaining southern portions of the village. The other sub-section of guns under SERGT. NEEDHAM lost touch, but regained it later, and crossed the river at 10.15 hrs, taking up a position in V.4.d.7.8.	
		10.15	No. 10 Section of "C" Coy under 2/Lt J. BAIRD moved forward, when the river was crossed in the early morning. Sgt. FOLLOWS. "C" Coy and sub-section of No.10 (since reported missing) was last seen in EAST outskirts of HAUSSY	
		14.00	At about 14.10 hrs the enemy made a counter-attack, and recaptured most of the ground gained EAST of the River in HAUSSY.	

Army Form C. 2118.

WAR DIARY
or
INTELLIGENCE SUMMARY.
(Erase heading not required.)

Place	Date	Hour	Summary of Events and Information	Remarks and references to Appendices
ST AUBERT.	16th		In response to the S.O.S. Signal, B Coy Battery in V 9 a. put down a barrage, and its fire is reported by 2/Lt A LINLEY to have assisted very greatly in saving the left flank of his position EAST of the River.	
		14.50	At 14.50 hrs. the sub section under Sgt NEEDHAM, in view of the progress made by the enemy, took up fresh positions on the WEST side of the River at V 9 d 6.6. to cover the valley in the direction of HAUSSY.	
			During the early part of the night, the enemy continued to counter-attack, and at	
		23.30	23.30 hrs., being nearly surrounded, the infantry commander decided to withdraw to the WEST side of the River.	
			The sub section of N° 8, after covering the retirement of the Infantry was also withdrawn. Nothing definite was ascertained regarding the RIGHT FLANK, but it is supposed that the enemy counter-attacked this flank from the SOUTH, working up the valley in a NORTH-WEST direction.	
		24.00	About dusk, 2/Lt J BAIRD, and the remaining sub section with 2 guns and 1 tripod withdrew to the WEST side of the River, and took up a position on the high ground in V 16 b.	
			8 O.R. evacuated sick to C.C.S. and struck off strength.	
			2/Lt MASON J.O. reported from BASE DEPOT, so taken on strength, and posted to 'A' Coy	D
			Lt. MORYOSEPH E.C. " " " " " " "	D
			2/Lt. JAMIESON A.C. " " " " " " "	D

Army Form C. 2118.

WAR DIARY
or
INTELLIGENCE SUMMARY.
(Erase heading not required.)

Place	Date	Hour	Summary of Events and Information	Remarks and references to Appendices
ST AUBERT.	17th	13.00	"B" Coy owing to heavy shelling moved their battery positions in V9a.8.3 to new positions in V9c.8.8 at 13.00 hrs	
		1700	At 17.00 hrs. "B", "C" and "D" Coys were relieved in positions – "A" Coy were relieved at 11.00 by 19TH BATTN. M.G.C.	
		20.30	"Relief of BATTN was complete by 20.30 hrs Companies marched independently to billets in EAST Outskirts of CAMBRAI.	
EAST outskirts of CAMBRAI	18th		LT JENNINGS. F.W. reported from BASE DEPOT, is taken on strength, and posted to C. Coy 2/LT MILNER A.B " " " " C "	
	19th		Day spent in cleaning billets – cleaning of guns and kit equipment. Refitting of clothing – Inspection of gun equipment. 5. O.R. rejoined from HOSPITAL and posted to Companies. 30. O.R. reported from BASE DEPOT, taken on strength, and posted to Companies	
	20th		Training programme commenced. Commanding Officer attended Companies Inspections by Coy Commanders. LT. COL H.R. de WETHERALL D.S.O M.C. GLOUCESTER REGT attached to this BATTN	
	21st		Training programme continued. 1.O.R admitted Fd Amb 1.O.R rejoined from HOSPITAL and posted to Company	

Army Form C. 2118.

WAR DIARY
or
INTELLIGENCE SUMMARY.
(Erase heading not required.)

Instructions regarding War Diaries and Intelligence Summaries are contained in F. S. Regs., Part II. and the Staff Manual respectively. Title pages will be prepared in manuscript.

Place	Date	Hour	Summary of Events and Information	Remarks and references to Appendices
EAST outskirts of CAMBRAI	22nd		Training programme continued	
	23rd		2. O.R. rejoined from Hospital.	
			1. O.R. admitted F.A. Amb.	
			1. O.R. joined from BASE DEPÔT, and posted to Coy	
			12. O.R. reported from A.H.T.D. are taken on strength, and posted to Companies	
			Training programme continued.	
	24th		2/Lt. E. O'KELLY reported from BASE DEPÔT, is taken on strength, and posted to D Coy	
			50 O.R. reported from BASE DEPÔT, are taken on strength, and posted to Companies	
			Training programme continued	
			2/Lt. HUTCHING A.V reported from BASE DEPOT, taken on strength, and posted to Coy	
			2/Lt. MOBBERLEY E.	
	25th		B Coy co-operated in TACTICAL SCHEME with 72nd Inf. Bde	
			Other Companies carried out daily programme of training	
			Battn. moved from EAST outskirts of CAMBRAI to billets in ST AUBERT	
ST AUBERT	26th		Training programme continued.	
	27th		Training programme continued.	
	28th		Training programme continued.	
	29th		Training programme included :— 13 a/ks. Squad Drill. Sectional Schemes, Elementary Gun Drill Digging and Recreational Exercises	

D. D. & L., London, E.C.
(10340. Wt.W53.03/P713. 750,000 3/18 E 2088 Forms C/2118/16.

Army Form C. 2118.

WAR DIARY
or
INTELLIGENCE SUMMARY.
(Erase heading not required.)

Instructions regarding War Diaries and Intelligence Summaries are contained in F. S. Regs., Part II. and the Staff Manual respectively. Title pages will be prepared in manuscript.

Place	Date	Hour	Summary of Events and Information	Remarks and references to Appendices
ST AUBERT	29th (cont)		2/Lt PARSONS H.E. reported from BASE DEPOT, is taken on strength, and posted to 'A' Coy	
			2/Lt TODD H. died in HOSPITAL (sickness)	
			2 O.R. evacuated to C.C.S. and struck off strength.	
	30th		2 O.R. reported from BASE DEPOT, and posted to Companies	
			Battalion Sports were held in the afternoon in field in outskirts of ST AUBERT	
			Training Programme included:- Firing, Gun and Squad Drill, Barrage Stoppages, Repacking Limbers, Physical Training, Combined Drill, and Recreational Training	
			2 O.R. admitted Fd. Amb.	
	31st		Training Programme:-	
			'A' Coy. Route March	
			'B' Revolver and Musketry Shooting at Range	
			'C' Tactical Scheme with 43rd Inf. Bde.	
			'D' Drill and Recreational Training	
			In the afternoon, the Battn. paraded for a lecture by Div Education Officer on "DEMOBILISATION"	
			1 O.R. admitted C.C.S. and struck off strength	
			Total Casualties during operations for month — 4 OFFRS. 135 OTHER RANKS.	

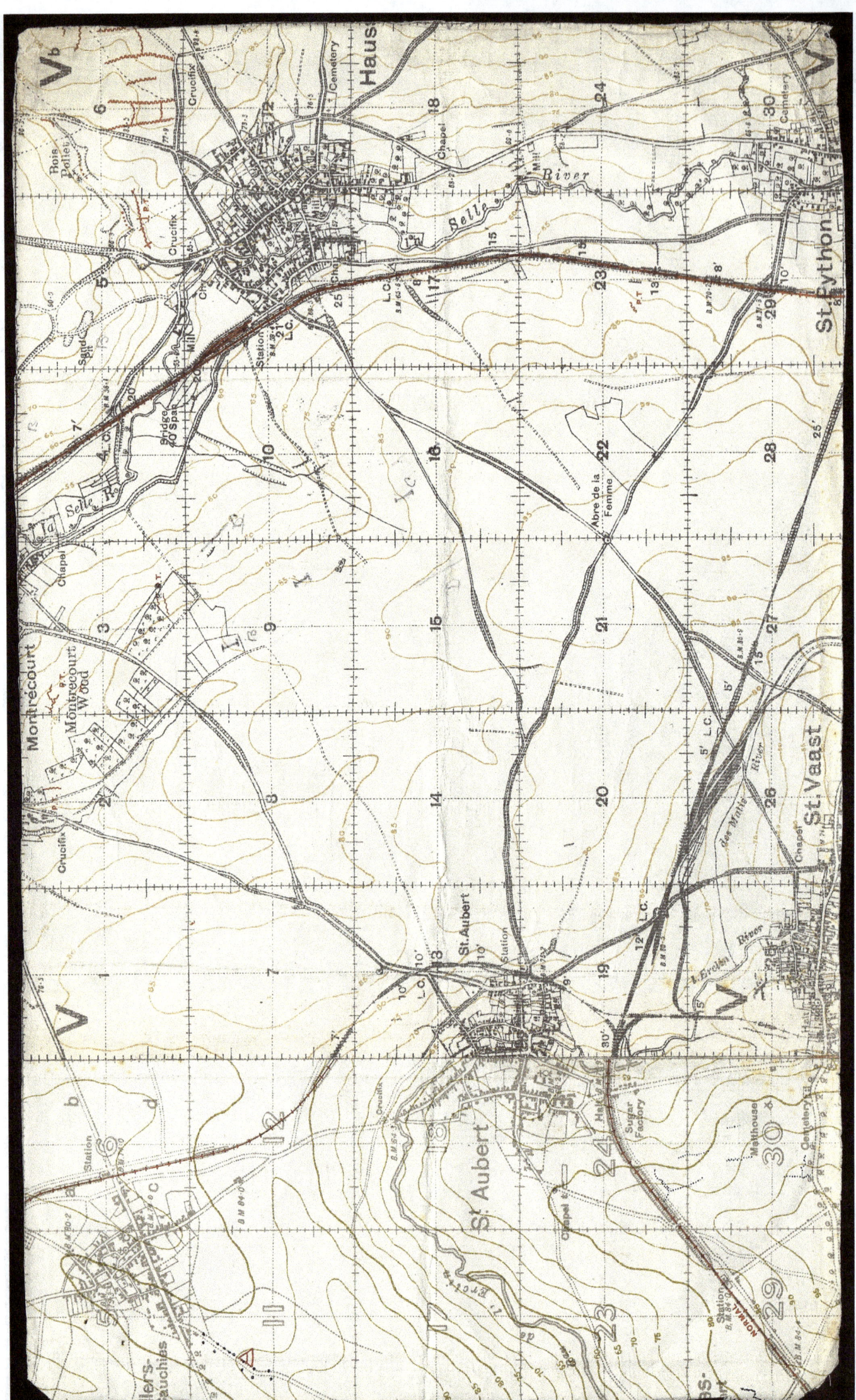

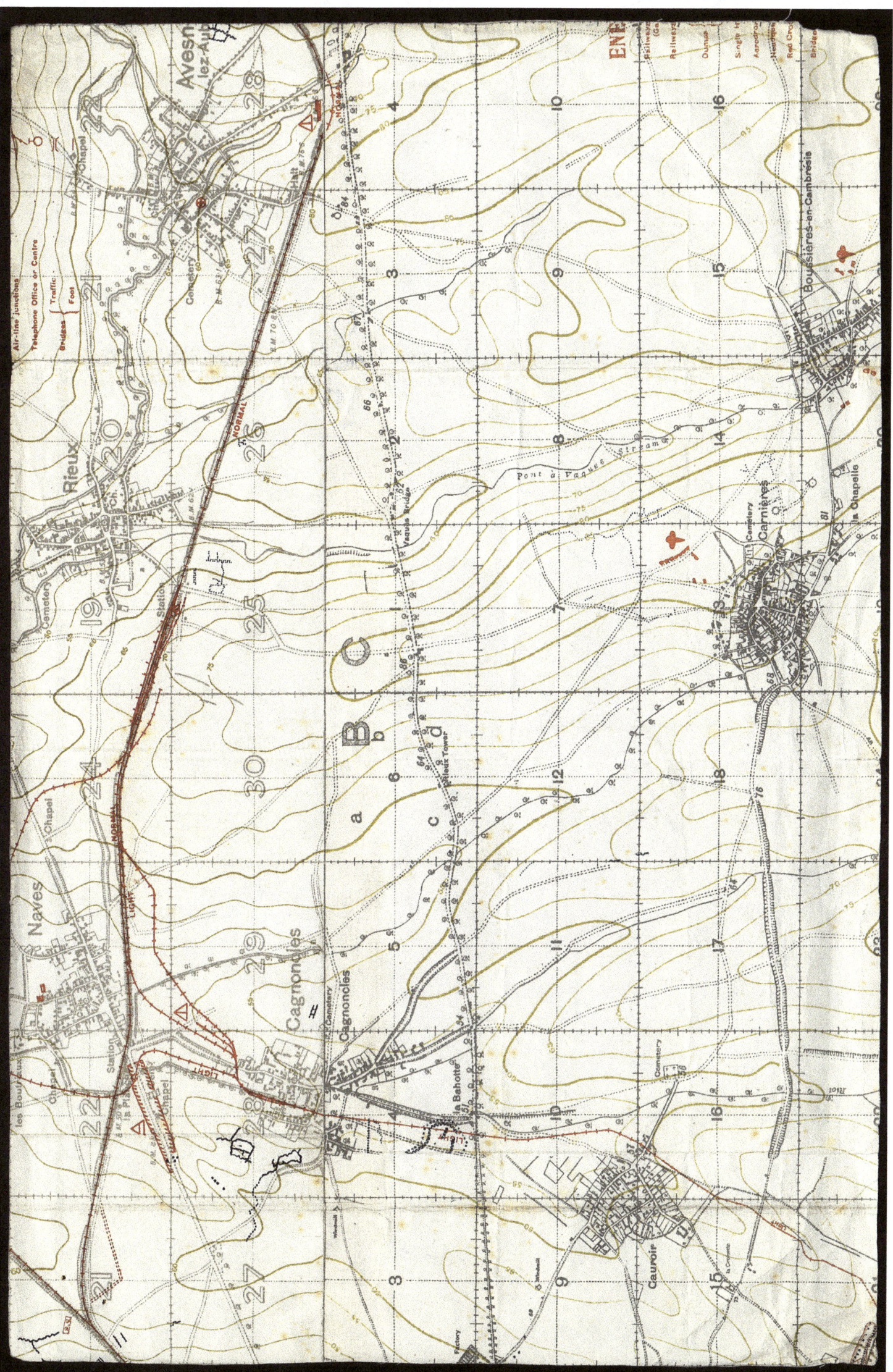

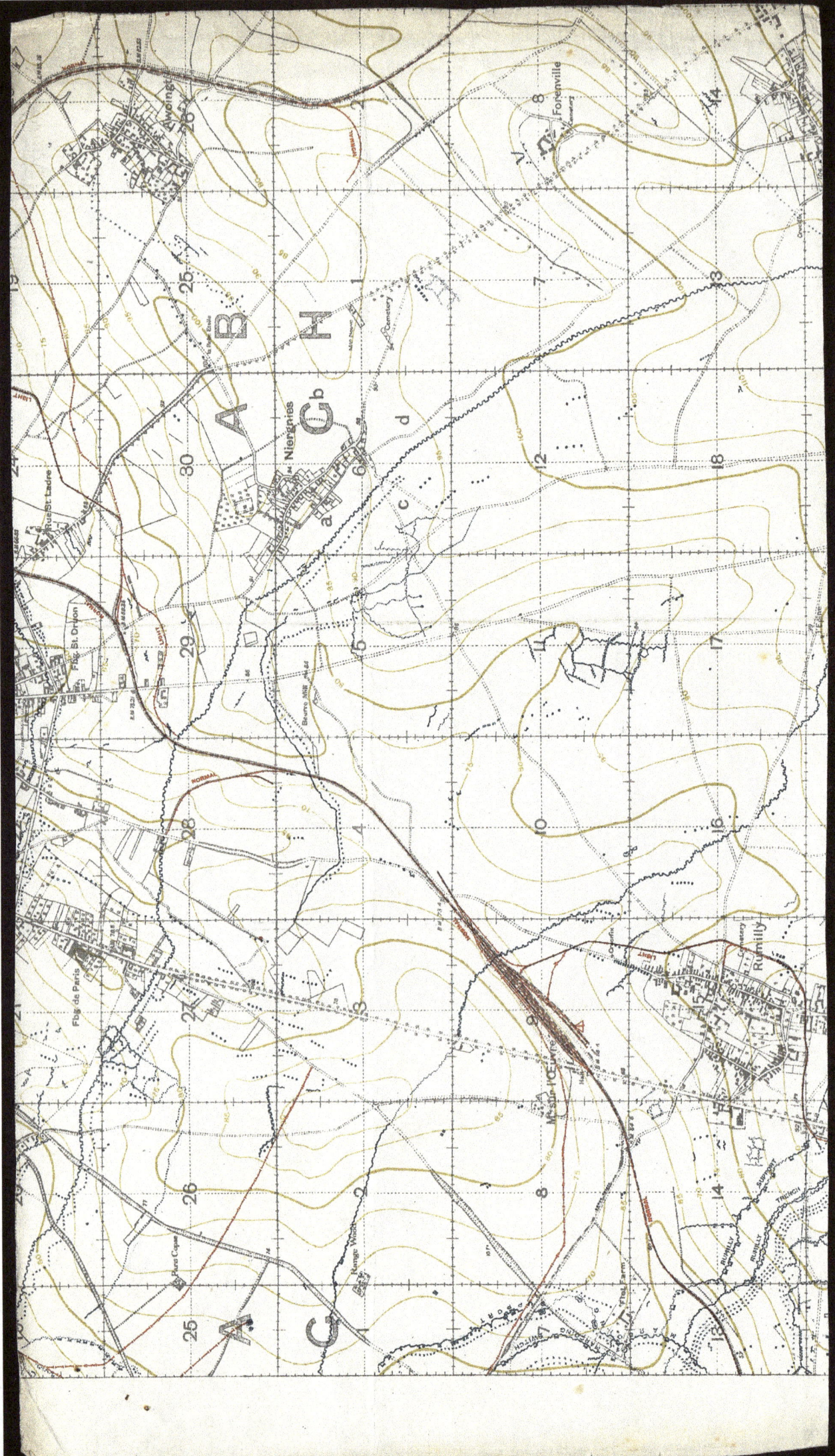

CONFIDENTIAL

WAR DIARY

OF

24TH BATTN. M.G.C.

FROM 1.11.'18   TO 30.11.'18

VOLUME 8

Army Form C. 2118.

WAR DIARY
INTELLIGENCE SUMMARY.
(Erase heading not required.)

Instructions regarding War Diaries and Intelligence Summaries are contained in F. S. Regs., Part II. and the Staff Manual respectively. Title pages will be prepared in manuscript.

Place	Date	Hour	Summary of Events and Information	Remarks and references to Appendices
ST AUBERT	1/11/18	1500	Orders were received from Division that 24th and 19th Divisions were relieved by 61st Division. A and B Coys transport moved to billets at Maurois. Lt Williams Depot Officer left for leave to U.K., and Lt Gardiner 9th from Div. HQ. Coy doing duty in his absence. 2 O.R. admitted C.C.S. and struck off strength.	
ST MARTIN	2/11/18	1500	Battalion H.Q., Heads of A + D Coys + B + C Coys (complete) left ST AUBERT at 1500 hours marching via HAUSSY to billets in ST MARTIN, B + C Coys remaining billets vacated by A + D Coys. The time of arrival at ST MARTIN was 1800 hrs. A Coy moved forward to relieve one of 6/St Batln. and D Coy moved to billets in BERMERAIN.	
		1800	A Coy now occupied following positions: One section in L 32 d 10.2.0, one section in R2 c 9.9, one section in R2 d 10.95 and one section in R2 central, Coy HQ being in Railway Embankment - R1 d 9.0. Patrols were sent on recon. of Coy front to Marlion near outskirts of MARESCHES to further the left flank of the 73rd I.B. North. Hostile shelling was experienced during the night resulting in 4 O.R's being slightly wounded and gassed and one O.R. put out of action.	
SEPMERIES	3/11/18	1000	At 1000 hours news was received that the enemy was withdrawing and	
		1400	at 1400 hours Batln. HQ. moved forward with the 73rd Infantry Brigade to SEPMERIES. (Rest Batln. N.R. had been established at BERMERAIN Q22 c.3.6. at 1000 hours)	S.B.
		1600	At 1600 hours A Company moved forward to billets in the Eastern outskirts of MARESCHES. Meanwhile further news came through that the enemy had retired from JENLAIN and VILLERS-POL. At 1630 hours	
MARESCHES		1630	Batln. HQ. moved forward to billets in MARESCHES B and C Companies stayed in billets in BERMERAIN. D company received orders to move forward to MARESCHES and to take up positions in high ground east of MARESCHES	

WAR DIARY
INTELLIGENCE SUMMARY.

Army Form C. 2118.

Place	Date	Hour	Summary of Events and Information	Remarks and references to Appendices
MARESCHES	3/11/18		in L.27a, L.28c, and MAISON BLANCHE and L.23d near LE CORON via VILLERS POL. "A" Company sustained casualties during move to MARESCHES and one other gun was put out of action. MAJOR DAVIES, C.G., M.C., reported from BASE DEPÔT and was taken on strength being posted to "D" Company. LT. A.M. COOKE and 2 O.R. proceeded to attend CORPS GAS SCHOOL (Course). 2/LT A. LINLEY and 2 O.R. rejoined from course at CORPS GAS SCHOOL. 16 O.R. (including 6 Cat:gry(B men) reported from BASE DEPÔT and being taken on strength were posted to companies.	
	4/11/18	0530	Casualties (up to 1800 hours):- 8 O.R. wounded, 15 O.R. struck off strength, admitted Field Ambulance. 5 O.R. admitted Field Ambulance. At 05.30 hours the 73rd Infantry Brigade attacked. "A" Company were detailed to support the attack. The first two sections on moving off came under very heavy shell fire and sustained several casualties to animals. One section reached their guns to protect the right flank of the 9th Royal Sussex Regiment. The positions being in G.26.e facing South East to fire across the valley in front. Two guns were placed to cover the western outskirts of WARGNIES-LE-PETIT and brisk effectually on any parties	ISB

WAR DIARY
or
INTELLIGENCE SUMMARY.
(Erase heading not required.)

Army Form C. 2118.

Place	Date	Hour	Summary of Events and Information	Remarks and references to Appendices
MARESCHES	4/11/18		of the march.	
		0645	One section of "A" Coy taking advantage of the mist found behind the second wave of the attack had arrived in the BRICKFIELDS at 06.45 hours. 2 guns of this section moved to about G.26.b.6.4.5 behind the front towards WERGNIES-LE-GRAND. The remaining section of "A" Company moved to position in BRICKFIELDS covering	
		0730	then at 0730 hours. "B" Company moved forward to support the attack. Two guns after incurring much machine gun fire were eventually brought into action in G.26.d.4.9; one of these guns fired direct into the enemy, raising in G.21.b and G.21.d. These two guns were pushed forward with the infantry and good targets were obtained. L/Cpl. Martin did excellent work he was slamming the gun when 3 of the crew were stranded causing up to within twenty feet of the gun. With great presence of mind he drew his revolver and shot 6 leading men, then dropping down beside the gun loaded it and fired, killing or wounding the remainder of the patrol.	S.S
		1800	At 1800 hours "D" Company moved into billets in JENLAIN. "C" Company now attached to the 13th MIDDLESEX, who were attacking	

WAR DIARY
INTELLIGENCE SUMMARY.
(Erase heading not required.)

Army Form C. 2118.

Place	Date	Hour	Summary of Events and Information	Remarks and references to Appendices
MARESCHES	4/11/18		On the left to capture WARGNIES-LE-GRAND. One section sent forward to give gun covering fire and commenced when the village was in our hands. Forward busk two sections went forward to sunken road in G.22.a to cover the remr as the situation was rather obscure. At 2200 hours another section pushed forward to Eastern outskirts of WARGNIES-LE-GRAND to co-operate with 7th ROYAL SUSSEX. Also guns taking up positions in G.22.b.1.1 and G.28.c.7.2.	
		2200	B Coy moved up to SEPMERIES for the night. A Coy H.Q. had moved at 1245 hours from BERMERAIN to SEPMERIES via SEPMERIES arriving in billets at LE CORONS for the night. Battalion H.Q. moved into billets at LE CORONS for the night. Casualties:- 2/Lt. A.B. MILNER died in action, 2/Lt. 50 KELLY wounded and struck off strength. 4 O.R. killed in action, 3 O.R. wounded in action, 3 O.R. missing. 3 O.R. evacuated as B.C.'s and struck off strength accordingly. 1 O.R. returned from Field Ambulance.	O.B.
LE CORONS	5/11/18	0500	At 0500 hours the 17th Infantry Brigade passed through the 73rd Infantry Brigade when WARGNIES-LE-GRAND and WARGNIES-LE-PETIT were in our hands.	
		0730	At 0730 hours "D" Coy. received orders to support the advance of the	

Place	Date	Hour	Summary of Events and Information	Remarks and references to Appendices
LE CORONS	5/10/14	0730	17th Infantry Brigade. Two sections left TENLAIN at 0745 hours to follow in close support of advancing infantry. The remainder of the company went forward with Brigade Headquarters. One Section came under heavy shell fire in H.25 a.9.9 and went - 3 miles. This section advanced to cross-roads in A200 and obtained direct fire on an enemy in ST WAAST and in H.21 a and 15. Most of this firing was done from the top corner of horses. One section pushed forward and observed an enemy machine gun in the edge of the wood at H.21 c.9.3. On opening fire two belts at the enemy gun and silenced it. Another enemy machine gun was silenced a few minutes later, and of was then possible to bring the remainder of the Section into position on the top of the ridge giving an excellent field of fire over ST WAAST and another approaches also ground in H.21, H.27 and H.28. Another section of "D" Company moved forward to H.25 x 5.4 but did not arrive till owing to the action sweeping all the routes by shell fire. These guns eventually came into action on the ridge in H.26 b on the left of "B" Coy.s section forming a direct fire battery. The enemy's guns did excellent work firing continually on bodies of the enemy until evening. At 2000 hours in Farragi moved fired to evacuate	N.B

WAR DIARY
INTELLIGENCE SUMMARY.
(Erase heading not required.)

Army Form C. 2118.

Place	Date	Hour	Summary of Events and Information	Remarks and references to Appendices
LE COROUS	5/11/18		forcing a crossing of the river in ST WAAST himself. "A" company had remained in their position until 0800 hours when they moved into billets in WARGNIES-LE-GRAND. "B" company moved in rear of the 72nd Brigade from MARESCHES and HARPIES POL to WARGNIES LE GRAND where they billeted for the night. "C" company also assembled in WARGNIES LE PETIT and later moved into billets in G.30.c.2.2. Battalion Headquarters moved forward into billet in La BOIS CRETTE Rear Headquarters moved from MARESCHES to G.19.d.3.6. on main VALENCIENNES road between JENLAIN and WARGNIES-LE-GRAND.	
LE BOIS CRETTE	6/11/18	1100	"A" company found an outpost line in WARGNIES-LE-GRAND and "B" company at 1100 hours "B" company moved to LE PLAT DE BOIS to relieve "D" company. Sections of "B" company were disposed as follows:— 1 section in H.20.c.55.40 1 " " H.20.c.30.37 2 sections " H.26.a.60.40. "C" company also assembled in the advance of the 17th Infantry Brigade and in position at H.15.c.6.2 and one section at H.28.c.2.2. Then sections hold carriage at 11:00 hours.	O.B.

WAR DIARY
INTELLIGENCE SUMMARY.

Army Form C. 2118.

(Erase heading not required.)

Place	Date	Hour	Summary of Events and Information	Remarks and references to Appendices
LA BOIS CRETTE	6/11/18	1700	Relief of "D" Company by "B" Company completed by 1700 hours upon relief "D" Company moved into billets in LA BOIS CRETTE. Casualties: 6 O.R. wounded in action. 1 O.R. injured from fall. Ambulance	
	7/11/18		"B" Company having been ordered to support the 72nd Infantry Brigade attack on BAVAY on the morning of the 7th, "C" Company first having to support the advance after which the advanced Infantry had moved forward the Company moved into billets in ST WAAST. "A" Company moved up at 1500 hours to billets in FACTORY in H.24 central. Headquarters meanwhile had pushed forward with Advanced Brigade H.Q. and established in HOTEL DE FAISAN BAVAY for the night.	
BAVAY			"B" Company was disposed as follows:— One section in H.15.c.90.20 firing barrage in support of R.W. KENTS, 2 sections in H.36.a.2.8 in support of the E. SURREYS. One section also went to H.28.c.5.7 in support of the E. SURREYS moving to the Railway. Movement was rendered difficult, bridge at H.29.a being blown up, little opposition by the enemy was being encountered and our forward actions were following in close support to the leading infantry. Forward section moved	O.R.

Army Form C. 2118.

WAR DIARY
or
INTELLIGENCE SUMMARY.
(Erase heading not required.)

Place	Date	Hour	Summary of Events and Information	Remarks and references to Appendices
BAVAY	7/11/18		through BAVAY and the W.KENTS and dug in at I.21.b and I.21.d during the night of the 7th-8th Nov. One section with the E SURREYS moved up and stayed the night with them at I.20.d 5.1. The remaining two sections moved forward with the E SURREYS to positions ready to support them if a/c clearing a way through KNIGHT thicket two sections moved into positions at I.25.a 90.95 for the night. "D" Coy. remained in billets in LA BOIS CRETÉ	E SURREYS
LONGUEVILLE	8/11/18	09.30	At 09.30 "A" Coy. (less two M.G.s) took up positions moved forward and the remainder of the Company moved forward to LONGUEVILLE. At about the same time the advance was resumed, the enemy having withdrawn a considerable distance to an approximate line of the railway at FEIGNES. A Company was attached to the W.KENTS and E SURREYS in following and operated along road in I.22.a, I.22.b, central and I.22.a. One section took up position whilst truck about I.20.b.9.m "C" Section in Sucrerie moved to I.26.b.9.2 and one section in reserve at I.25.a 3.9. "B" Company marched to LONGUEVILLE during the morning and billeted there for the night. "C" Company moved up to billets in BAVAY for the night. "D" Coy. moved up to billets in LONGUEVILLE.	N.B.

Army Form C. 2118.

WAR DIARY
or
INTELLIGENCE SUMMARY.
(Erase heading not required.)

Place	Date	Hour	Summary of Events and Information	Remarks and references to Appendices
LONGUEVILLE	8/11/18		Reconnaissance moved from LA BOIS CRETE to BAVAY 12.5 a 95.15	
	9/11/18		To BAVAY and billets at N.B. and D Company Breakfast 10.R. companies. The advance was resumed without artillery preparation. Two sections of 'D' company went forward as the advance guard infantry, one section with the E. SURREYS and one with the N. STAFFS. The remainder of the company followed along the main road to FEIGNIES. The forward sections pushed forward and gained the MONS–MAUBEUGE Rd & stayed on the infantry on high ground in A22b and K23a. The remainder of the company advanced along the main road through REVEAU, FORT LEVEAU and established company HQ in F9c HERON PONTAINE. Enemy were encountered up to this point & two guns were pushed forward and the infantry to outskirts on high ground in K24 & 95.10. These two guns did good work and obtained direct fire on enemy in K20 and K21 until almost three more guns were pushed forward to this time before dark. The guns having been retained from the rear until	LAB

WAR DIARY / INTELLIGENCE SUMMARY

Army Form C. 2118.

Place	Date	Hour	Summary of Events and Information	Remarks and references to Appendices
FEIGNIES	9/11/18		On receiving from the company were brought forward to high ground on the MONS-MAUBEUGE RD W of K.22 a and K.22.8. Coy H.Q. Tanks and 2 Coys infantry bridgehead through enemy and established in K.21.158. "B" Company were ordered to reinforce 73rd Infantry Brigade who were moving through 72nd Infantry Brigade, and to move forward in the direction of LES BAS YENTS. The company was subjected to shell fire, one section and R.W.W. H.Q'rs and Company Headquarters and 2 sections reached Brigade Headquarters. Little opposition was encountered not at	LB
		1000	1000 hours Company headquarters were established at J.17.6.9.3. One of the sections moved forward in advance to assist. Enemy held the NORTHAMPTON REGIMENT but no attack was encountered. During the night of 9th–10th the enemy was reported to have	
			Our section at BETTIGNIES / Coy " FORT DES SARTS / Two " MOMBESON PARK One O.R. returned to field ambulance.	

WAR DIARY or INTELLIGENCE SUMMARY

Army Form C. 2118.

Place	Date	Hour	Summary of Events and Information	Remarks and references to Appendices
BAVAY	10/11/18		Positions of yesterday were maintained until relieved by the 20th Batt. M.G.C. Battn. Headquarters moved back to HOTEL DU SION, BAVAY. "A" Company marched back to billets in LOUVIGNIES BAVAY. "B" Company marched to billets vacated by "C" Coy in LONGUEVILLE, "C" Coy to billets in LOUVIGNIES BAVAY. "D" Company moved to billets "B" FEIGNIES vacated by "A" Coy. Total Casualties during operations 2 Officers & 9 O.R.s	
	11/11/18		Hostilities ceased at 11.00 hours. All day troops staying put on line reached at Cost Fire. LT-COL. N.I. WHITTYDALE left for duty in England. LT-COL. H.E. WETHERALL, DSO, M.C. assumed command of 2nd Batt. M.G.C. 40 O.R. reported from Base hospital — posted to companies. 1 O.R. admitted field ambulance. 1 O.K. rejoined from HOSPITAL. 3 O.R. rejoined from field ambulance. 2 O.R. struck off strength — reported sick	W.R.

WAR DIARY
INTELLIGENCE SUMMARY.
(Erase heading not required.)

Army Form C. 2118.

Place	Date	Hour	Summary of Events and Information	Remarks and references to Appendices
BAVAY	12/12/18		MAJOR C.G. DAVIES M.C. assumes command of "B" Company. Battery handed over to "B" Company.	
	13/12/18		5 O.R. evacuated sick to C.C.S. and struck off strength accordingly. 3 O.R. returned from Hospital and reposted to companies. 3 O.R. admitted FIELD AMBULANCE. 1 O.R. reposted from Hospital.	
	14/12/18		2 O.R. struck off strength	
	15/12/18		Battalion paraded for analysis by LT-COL. H.E. de R. WETHERAL D.S.O., M.C.	
	16/12/18		LT. R.W. BROWN proceeded to U.K. for tour of duty and attached M.G.R. 2 O.R. admitted 2 FIELD AMBULANCE.	
WARGNIES-LE-PETIT.	17/12/18	11.00	Battalion moved from BAVAY at 11.00 hours to WARGNIES-LE-PETIT. 5 O.R. admitted to FIELD AMBULANCE. 51 O.R. returned from BASE DEPOT etc. on strength and posted to Companies.	

Army Form C. 2118.

WAR DIARY
INTELLIGENCE SUMMARY

(Erase heading not required.)

Place	Date	Hour	Summary of Events and Information	Remarks and references to Appendices
DENAIN	19/7/18	0730	The battalion moved from WARGNIES-LE-PETIT at 07.30 hours via VILLERS-POL, MARESCHES, MAING, to DENAIN arriving there at 03.00 hours approximately.	
ANICHE	19/7/18	0300 10.40	The battalion moved from DENAIN at 10.40 hours proceeding via ABSCON to ANICHE arriving there at 01.00 hours. Prior to entering ANICHE the battalion marched past the DIVISIONAL COMMANDER previous to entering the town. 4 O.R. admitted to C.C.S. and struck off strength. 6 O.R. rejoined from HOSPITAL. 1 O.R. admitted to Field Ambulance. 4 O.R. rejoined from Field Ambulance.	N.B.
	20/7/18		Battalion HeadQuarters at ANICHE billet No 26 RUE D'ABBEY. Recreational training carried out by companies. 13 O.R. struck off strength evacuated to C.C.S. 1 O.R. admitted to Field Ambulance. 10 R. struck off strength and evacuated to C.C.S. 7 OR detached for duty at H.Q. Letter G.H.Q. (these men were category B3 and were now returned for duty in France).	
	21/7/18			

WAR DIARY
INTELLIGENCE SUMMARY

Army Form C. 2118.

Place	Date	Hour	Summary of Events and Information	Remarks and references to Appendices
ANICHE	22/11/18		1 O.R. reported from C.C.S. taken on strength. 3 O.R. struck off strength - evacuated C.C.S. 1 O.R. admitted Field Ambulance.	
	23/11/18		1 O.R. admitted to Field Ambulance.	
	24/11/18		10 O.R. reported from BASE DEPOT taken on strength and posted to companies	N.B.
			3 O.R. admitted to Field Ambulance. 1 O.R. struck off strength - evac. of duty in U.K. 1 O.R. struck off strength - evacuated to C.C.S.	
	25/11/18		60 O.R. reported from BASE DEPOT taken on strength. 1 O.R. struck off strength - evacuated to C.C.S. 2 O.R. admitted to Field Ambulance	
SAMEON	26/11/18	0800	The battalion marched from ANICHE to SAMEON via SOMAIN, MARCHIENNES, BEUVRY, and LANDAS, time of departure 0800 hours, headquarters established at B.11.(c).4.2.70 at 1500 hours. 1 O.R. admitted to Field Ambulance.	

WAR DIARY
INTELLIGENCE SUMMARY

Army Form C. 2118.

1st

Place	Date	Hour	Summary of Events and Information	Remarks and references to Appendices
SAMEON	27/11/18		1 OR rejoined from C.C.S. and posted to company 6 OR struck off strength on evacuation to C.C.S. 1 OR admitted to FIELD AMBULANCE	
	28/11/18		9 OR admitted FIELD AMBULANCE 2/Lt: E.J.K. HUNT admitted FIELD AMBULANCE	
	29/11/18		4 OR rejoined from BASE DEPOT taken on strength and posted to companies 4 OR admitted FIELD AMBULANCE	19.15
	30/11/18		2 OR struck off strength on evacuation 7 OR struck off strength debited to Divisional M.G. SECTION G.H.Q. (on Nov 2/18) 1 OR struck off strength to BASE DEPOT 1 OR — to TRANSPORTATION TROOPS BASE DEPOT 2 OR admitted FIELD AMBULANCE	

D.A.A.G.
  24th. Division.

  Herewith attached War Diary for month of December 1918.

> 24TH BATTALION,
> MACHINE GUN
> CORPS.
>
> No. M.G. 76
> Date 6.3.'19

5. 3. 19.

H.H.Kolman(?)

Capt and Adjt.
24th. Batt. M.G.Corps.

SECRET AND CONFIDENTIAL

VOLUME 9.

24 Bn M G Corps
№ 10

WAR DIARY FOR MONTH OF DECEMBER 1918.

[signature] Lieut Col.

Commanding 24th. Machine Gun Corps.

Army Form C. 2118.

WAR DIARY
~~INTELLIGENCE SUMMARY~~
(Erase heading not required.)

Instructions regarding War Diaries and Intelligence Summaries are contained in F. S. Regs., Part II. and the Staff Manual respectively. Title pages will be prepared in manuscript.

Place	Date	Hour	Summary of Events and Information	Remarks and references to Appendices
SAMEON	Dec 1st		Major C. P. Mons struck off strength	
	2nd		1 OR Struck Sick off strength	
			2 ORs admitted F.A.	
	3rd		1 OR taken on strength	
			6 ORs invalided to C.C.S. 30-11-18 returned off strength	
			YoRs - 29-11-18 -	
			1 OR struck off strength	
			2 ORs admitted to C.C.S.	
	4th		10 ORs admitted to F.A.	
	5th		5 ORs struck off strength	
			2 ORs admitted to F.A.	
	6th		1 OR taken on strength	
			11 ORs struck off strength	
	7th		6 ORs taken on strength	
			2 ORs admitted F.A.	
	8th		3 ORs struck off strength	
	11th		1 OR reported from hospital in taken on strength	
			2 ORs evacuated to C.C.S. now struck off strength	

WAR DIARY
or
INTELLIGENCE SUMMARY.
(Erase heading not required.)

Army Form C. 2118.

Instructions regarding War Diaries and Intelligence Summaries are contained in F. S. Regs., Part II. and the Staff Manual respectively. Title pages will be prepared in manuscript.

Place	Date	Hour	Summary of Events and Information	Remarks and references to Appendices
SAMEON	Dec 12d		1 O.R. struck off strength	
			4 O.Rs evacuated to F.A.	
	14d		2 ORs transferred to O.K. for dembly from rest stats. Struck off strength accordingly	
			1 O.R. admitted to F.A. Capt Robinson to Boyelerts leave Cambrije	
	15d		3 OR struck off strength	
	17d		3 OR struck off strength	
			2 Lieut Burnett admitted to serve on Court of Enquiry Offrs on 15.12.18	
			Lieut the Palmer proceed to on Duct Duty in ref to re between	
	18d	13.00	Battalion moved in Tournai - full dress	
TOURNAI	20d	08.00	1 OR struck off strength	
			1 O.R. & 3 ORs transferred to hospital returned 10 units Struck off strength	
			1 OR admitted CCS on sick / strength	
	24d		1 OR evacuated to OK for demobilization no struck off strength	
	26d		1 OR admitted CCS no struck / strength	
	31d		22 fine 1 OR / sick & wounded & sick - Conv & Kpt Comng R/M Granny School	
	31d		1 O.R. admitted to F.A.	

SECRET & CONFIDENTIAL

The D.A.G.
    3rd Echelon.

        Forwarded herewith War Diary for the month of
January 1919.

                                            Capt & Adjt.
1.3.19   for O.C. 24th Battn. M.G.Corps.

VOLUME No. 10

SECRET & CONFIDENTIAL.

WAR DIARY FOR THE MONTH OF JANUARY 1919.

[signature]
Lieut - Colonel.
Commanding 24th Battalion Machine Gun Corps.

WAR DIARY or INTELLIGENCE SUMMARY

Army Form C. 2118.

2/Lt B. MGC

Place	Date	Hour	Summary of Events and Information	Remarks and references to Appendices
TOURNAI	Jan 1st		2/Lt B took promoted to Rank of Lieut	
	2nd		2 ORs reported from Base Depot & are taken on strength	
	3rd		3 ORs evacuated to 6.68 & are struck off strength	
	5th		1 OR rejoined from Hospital & is taken on strength	
	6th		1 OR admitted to ─	
			2 OR admitted to ─	
			1 OR evacuated to CCS & struck off strength	
	7th	9.45	2/Lt E Ford proceeded to UK on educating officer	
	8th		6 ORs proceeded to UK for Demobilization & are struck off strength	
			Battalion made up their first Property to Lieut	
			2 ORs returned from Field Depot & are taken on strength	
			3 ORs proceeded to UK for Demobilization & are struck off strength	
	9th		2 OR admitted to F.A.	
			1 OR Demobilized (authority Home Records No Z & (50) 44	
	11th		9 ORs reported from Base Depot & are taken on strength	
			10 ORs proceeded to UK for Demobilization & are struck off strength	
			1 OR admitted to F.A.	
	13th		3 ORs reported from Base Depot & are taken on strength	

WAR DIARY
or
INTELLIGENCE SUMMARY.

Army Form C. 2118.

Place	Date	Hour	Summary of Events and Information	Remarks and references to Appendices
TOURNAI	13th		2/Lt Baker F. struck off strength. 2/Lt Hunt E.T.T. struck off strength.	
	14th	0945	3 O.Rs. evacuated to C.C.S. & are struck off strength. A/Cpl Unysogh proceeded to Demobilization Camp for duty as struck off. 1 O.R. admitted to F.A. Battalion Parade in Place du Parc.	
	15th		2 O.Rs. proceeded to U.K. for Demobilization & are struck off strength 12/1/19	
		1302		14/1/19
	16th		1 O.R. admitted F.A. Capt. Robinson wounded. Military band. 3 O.R. proceed to U.K. for Demobilization & are struck off strength	
	17th		1 O.R. evacuated C.C.S. & struck off strength. A/Cpl Knock returned from conducting duty	
	18th		38 O.R. admitted to Hospital whilst in town & are struck off strength Battalion Parade in Place du Parc.	
	21st	0945	Lt J.C. Evans, Lt J. Williams & W.O.R. Maffen proceeded to U.K. for Demobilization & are struck off strength.	
	22nd		8 O.Rs. proceeded to U.K. for Demobilization & struck off strength. 12 O.R. proceeded to U.K. for Demobilization & struck off strength 1 O.R. proceed to Dispersal Camp & struck off strength	

Army Form C. 2118.

WAR DIARY
or
INTELLIGENCE SUMMARY.
(Erase heading not required.)

Instructions regarding War Diaries and Intelligence Summaries are contained in F. S. Regs., Part II. and the Staff Manual respectively. Title pages will be prepared in manuscript.

Place	Date	Hour	Summary of Events and Information	Remarks and references to Appendices
TOURNAI	23rd		RSM Dane, CQMS Wolstenholmes } award Meritorious Service Medal. Sgt Horton	
			2/Lt JKings proceed to UK for Demobilization & is struck off strength.	
			2 ORs admitted CCS and are struck of strength.	
			2 ORs admitted FA	
	24th		1 OR rejoined from CCS & is taken on strength	
	27th		2/W A Hutchinson proceeds to UK for Demobilization & is struck off strength	
			1 ORs	
			4 OR at ett Div HQ & is struck off strength.	
	29th		2 ORs evacuated CCS & are struck off strength	
			Capt James GD, Lt Cobb HB } wounded to UK for Demob & are struck off strength	
	30th		12 OR	
			1 OR reported from Base Depot & is taken on Strength	
			1 OR admitted FA	
			2/Lt Purcell the 4/Lt Brayman & 2/Lt Roger proceeds [unit]	

SECRET AND CONFIDENTIAL

WAR DIARY FOR MONTH OF FEBRUARY 1919.

[signature] Lieut Col.
Commanding 24th. BATT. MACHINE GUN CORPS.

Army Form C. 2118.

WAR DIARY
or
INTELLIGENCE SUMMARY.
(Erase heading not required.)

Instructions regarding War Diaries and Intelligence Summaries are contained in F. S. Regs., Part II. and the Staff Manual respectively. Title pages will be prepared in manuscript.

Place	Date	Hour	Summary of Events and Information	Remarks and references to Appendices
TOURNAI	FEB. 1st		Lt. F.F.Fick. J. proceeded UK for Demobulisation	
	2nd		9. ORs proceeded to UK for demobulisation	
			1. OR. demobilised while in UK.	
	3		29. OR proceeded to UK for demobulisation.	
	4		2. OR. struck of strength having been in hospital over 7 days — joined the F.F.C. Demobilisation HESDIN. 3-2-19.	
	5		1. OR. — demobilised while in UK.	
			2. OR. — evacuated to C.C.S ? ostruck of struck accordingly	
	6		1. OR. struck of strength having been in hospital over 7 days	
			Lt. A.R. Peskin proceeded to UK for demobulisation	
			20. ORs	
	7		Major J.S. Hayter assumed command of the Batt. on Lieut-Col. H.E. de R. Whitefeld D.S.O., M.C., proceeding on leave to UK.	
			18. ORs demobilised while in UK.	
			Major O.G. Davis M.C. proceeded to UK for Demobulisation	
	10		30. ORs proceeding to UK for demobulisation	
			1. OR evacuated to C.C.S. 8 9 struck of strength.	
			30. PR. proceeded to UK for demobulisation.	
			Lt J. Bund. + 2Lt. F.B. Williams proceeded to UK for demobulisation	
			20. OR. proceeded to UK for demobulisation.	
	12		Lt W. Bridgeman + 2Lt. a. C. Jamieson proceeded to UK for demob.	
			26. OR proceeded to UK for Demobilisation	

Army Form C. 2118.

WAR DIARY
or
INTELLIGENCE SUMMARY.

(Erase heading not required.)

Instructions regarding War Diaries and Intelligence Summaries are contained in F. S. Regs., Part II. and the Staff Manual respectively. Title pages will be prepared in manuscript.

Place	Date	Hour	Summary of Events and Information	Remarks and references to Appendices
TOURNAI	13		3. O.R. rejoined from Hospital & are taken on strength.	
	14.		1. O.R. evacuated to 6.6.5. & struck off strength.	
			Capt. J. Harris & Lieut. J. Logan proceed to U.K. for demobilisation 13-2-19.	
	15.		21. O.R. proceeded to U.K. for demobilisation, 13-2-19.	
			Capt. L.D. Buxton - - - 14-2-19.	
	16.		5. O.R. demobilised while in U.K.	
	17.		2. O.R. admitted to Field Ambulance. 16 - 17/2/19	
	18.		1. O.R. reported from C.C.S. 13-2-19 & taken on strength.	
			1. O.R. evacuated to C.C.S. & struck off strength 15-2-19.	
			1. O.R. admitted to Field Ambulance	
	20.		2. O.R. proceeded to U.K. for demobilisation on 8-2-19.	
			1. O.R. reported from 6.B.S. & is taken on strength.	
	21.		1. O.R. evacuated to C.C.S. & is struck off strength.	
			Lt. W.A. Rogers proceeded to U.K. for Demob. & is struck off strength 2-2-19	
			Lt. G.W. Stone & Lt. H. Rodgers proceeded to U.K. for duty as conducting officers. (15 & 21 inst.)	
	22		2. O.R. demobilised while in U.K. (16 & 21 inst.)	
	24		2. O.R. taken on strength at Corps Base Camp. from 21-2-19.	
	25.		Lt. A.H. Tooke proceeded to Corps Base Camp for conducting duty.	
			1. O.R. admitted to Field Ambulance 21-2-19.	

Army Form C. 2118.

WAR DIARY
or
INTELLIGENCE SUMMARY.
(Erase heading not required.)

Place	Date	Hour	Summary of Events and Information	Remarks and references to Appendices
TOURNAI	26		Lieut Col A.E. McDowell returned from leave to UK & assumed command of the Battalion	1337
	27		1 OR. struck off strength having been in hospital over 7 days	
			2 OR. admitted to Field Ambulance 27-2-19.	
	28		1 OR. admitted to F.A. & to Truck off strength	
			Major Purdy admitted to CCS. ?	

SECRET & CONFIDENTIAL

D.A.G.
G.H.Q. 3rd Echelon.

    Forwarded herewith War Diary for the month of
March 1919.

                     Captain & Adjutant.
                for O.C. 24th Battn M.G.Corps.

3.4.19

**24TH BATTALION.
MACHINE GUN
CORPS.**

No. M.G.352
Date

SECRET & CONFIDENTIAL.

24TH BATTALION MACHINE GUN CORPS.

WAR DIARY FOR THE MONTH OF MARCH 1919.

VOLUME 13

[signature]
Lieut Colonel
Commanding 24th Battn. M.G.Corps.

Army Form C. 2118.

WAR DIARY
or
INTELLIGENCE SUMMARY.
(Erase heading not required.)

Instructions regarding War Diaries and Intelligence Summaries are contained in F. S. Regs., Part II. and the Staff Manual respectively. Title pages will be prepared in manuscript.

Place	Date	Hour	Summary of Events and Information	Remarks and references to Appendices
TOURNAI	MARCH 1st		Summer time came into use at 23.00 hrs	
	2nd		2OR proceeded to No 7 Stationary Hospital	
	3rd		2OR evacuated CCS and struck off a'tength	
			1OR demobilised whilst on leave to UK 13.1.18	
	4th		4OR struck off a'tength (on CCS 2.3.19) 8OR proceeded to No 4 Base Remount Depot on ceasing of duty	
			1OR demobilised whilst on leave to UK 15.1.18	
	5th		1OR admitted CCS 2.3.19 & stuck off a'tength	
	6th		1OR admitted hospital. 5OR admitted CCS & struck off a'tength 5.3.19	
	7th		2/Lt Mc SAA returned to AMY DUMP TEMPLEUVE (FRANCE)	
			Lt DS LAUGHLAND proceeded on leave to UK. Lt. FH BURY returned from leave to UK. 1OR demobilised which on return to UK 21.1.19. 1OR demobilised whilst on leave to UK 6.3.19 & stuck off	
			came to UK 24.1.19. Major EM RUNTZ evacuated back to UK 6.3.19 & stuck off a'tength.	
	8th		6OR proceeded to Corps Remount Camp for demobilyn ha & an stuck off a'tength. 2OR admitted hospital	
			1OR evacuated to CCS 7.3.19 & struck off a'tength. 2/Lt. WESTHEAD returned from	
	9th		C/E church parade in the morning. 2OR admitted CCS & struck off a'tength	
	10th		Nil	
	11th		Lt. FH BURY proceeded to UK for duty & a'tength.	
	12th		70 X animals sent away to 103rd Bde AFA. 2/Lt. J WESTHEAD returned from leave to UK.	
	13th		1OR admitted hospital Lt. FS FRITH proceeded on leave to UK	
	14th		Major J GILBERT. C.G.C. MC assumed command of Bn on Lt Col WETHERALL DSO MC_I MAJOR HARREN	

WAR DIARY
or
INTELLIGENCE SUMMARY.
(Erase heading not required.)

Army Form C. 2118.

Place	Date	Hour	Summary of Events and Information	Remarks and references to Appendices
TOURNAI	MARCH 2nd		Summer time comes into use at 23.00 hrs. 2oR proceeded to No.1 Canadian Hospital Force man't sick.	
	3rd		2OR admitted CCS and struck off strength. 1OR admitted sick from leave + UR 10 1.18 1OR demobilised & hilton leave + UR 15.1.18	
	4th		4OR struck off strength (same res. 1.3.19) 8OR proceeded (S. No 4 Gen. Bose + Hlg-tm evac'n) strength	
	5th		1OR admitted CCS + s.o.s. - s'off strength	
	6th		1OR admitted hosp sick. 5OR admitted CCS + struck off strength 5.3.19.	
	7th		Col. McSAA returned to No 4 Dump temporarily (France) Lt DS LANGLAND proceed on leave to UK. Lt. F.H. Bury returned from leave to UK 9.1.19. 1OR admitted whilst on leave to UK + UK 24.1.19. Major E M RUNTZ evacuated sick + UK 63.19 & Struck off strength	
	8th		6OR proceeded to top Kingston Lanny for demobily 15 & sos struck off strength. 1OR vacated + CCS 7.3.19 + struck off str. 2OR admitted to CCS - s'off strength	
	9th 10th		C/C Church parade in the morning 2OR admitted CCS + struck off strength nil	
	11th		Lt. F H BURY proceeded to UK / s.o.s. + struck off strength	
	12th		70 x animals sent back to 108 Res AFA 3/11 8 W.O.S.+ DEAD returned from leave to UK	
	13th 14th		1OR admitted Hospital. Lt. FS FRITH proceeded on leave to UK. Major GILBERT CGC OC command summary the 2 other R Hetherick Dix.P? & Major HARPER	

WAR DIARY
INTELLIGENCE SUMMARY
(Erase heading not required.)

Army Form C. 2118.

Sheet II

Place	Date MARCH	Hour	Summary of Events and Information	Remarks and references to Appendices
TOURNAI	15th		proceeding on leave in Belgium. 3 OR proceeded to UK for demob. & are struck off strength.	
	16th		10 R demobilized whilst on leave in UK & struck off strength. 2/Lt E.A. MORBERLEY and servant returned from course.	
	17th		2/Lt L.A. MASON & 11 OR proceeded to UK for demob & are struck off strength Lt. T.H. RODGERS returned from leave in UK. 2 OR evacuated CCS & struck off strength. 1 Col WETHERALL returned from leave & assumed command of 7 Bn Tn. MAJOR HARPER returned from leave.	
	18th		Lt. P. KIMBER proceeded on leave to UK. LT S. PETRIE G.W. (MC) & COOKE A.M. returned from leave. 4 OR 15 'x' Group horses left Bagh for base. 2/Lt TIDY E.G. & 96 OR proceeded to/Jim 1st Bn M.G.C. & are struck off strength. 3 OR proceeded to Divnl. Transport Park at BAISIEUX.	
	19th		10 R reported from Base & taken on strength.	
	20th		Major J.S. HARPER M.C. proceeded to UK for duty in a struck off strength. 2 OR evacuated to CCS struck off strength 2/Lt LINLEY returned from leave in UK. 10R rejoined from Hospital & taken on strength	
	21st		6'2 horses left for base. All demobilizat'n leave etc having cancelled owing Threatened strikes in England.	
	22nd		10 R proceeded on leave countermanding to base. Lt D S LAUGHLAND returned from leave in UK	
	23rd		10 R rejoined from Hospital & taken on strength	

WAR DIARY
INTELLIGENCE SUMMARY

Army Form C. 2118.

Place	Date	Hour	Summary of Events and Information	Remarks and references to Appendices
TOURNAI	MARCH 15th		Proceeding Leave in Belgium	
	16th		10R demobility & whilst in Place — UK & a final f/strength. 2/Lt EA MONBERLEY and advance returned from course.	
			2/Lt LA MASON & 11OR proceeded to UK for demob & as a final f/strength. Lt. M. RODGERS returned from Base to UK. 20R proceeded CCS 3 for f/strength.	
	17th		Lt. WETHERALL returned from Leave L assumed command of 7 Bn Ths MAJOR HARPER returned from Leave.	
	18th		Lt P. KIMBER proceeded on Leave to UK. Lts PATRICK (MC) & COOKE RM returned from Leave. 2OR 2/Lt TIDY EC + 91OR proceeded to f/m. 15 x group from Left Battn Leave 30R proceeded & died Transport Park at	2OR
	19th	1/Bn 19C = as a final f/strength.	BAILIEUX	
	20th		10R up to f/m from Base x Return in f/st. Major JS HARPER proceeded to UK for appointment f/strength. 2OR demobbed 2/Lt LINDSAY L/cum for Leave — UK = 10R	
	21st		arrived from Hospital & Return in f/strength. 6.2 demob left both to the line. All demob/sgts Leave to have cancelled every Thursday & Return to England	
	22nd		10R proceeded on Leave to UK 1 to Ireland. 1 DS in Ireland returned from leave — UK.	
	23rd		10R reported from Hospital on Return in f/str.	

Army Form C. 2118.

Sheet III

WAR DIARY
or
INTELLIGENCE SUMMARY.
(Erase heading not required.)

Place	Date	Hour	Summary of Events and Information	Remarks and references to Appendices
TOURNAI	24th		nil	
	25th		70 OR proceeded to Corps Concentration Camp for dismot. 1 OR struck off strength. 2 OR proceeded to ETAPLES. 1 OR struck off strength. 127 mules sent to base.	
	26th		Battalion moved into billets at MARQUAIN. Paraded 15 O who's reached billets	
MARQUAIN	27th		6/16.30hrs. 10 OR evacuated CCS & struck off strength.	
	28th		10 OR returned from base conducting duty	
			Lt. P. KIMBER & 10 OR posted to 1st Bn 76C & struck off strength. 1 OR struck off strength whilst at COOKERY SCHOOL ETAPLES.	
	29th		Seven ORs and the following officers proceeded to join 1st Bn 76C today & are struck off strength. Lt (A/Capt) WOOD G.M.A., Lt (A/Capt) TRENT W.A. M.C.	
			Lt J.C. KNOTH Lt H.E. PARSONS M.C. 2/Lt A. LINLEY.	
			" D.S. LAUGHLAND " E.C. MORYOSEPH	
			" A.M. COOKE " G.W. PETRIE M.C.	
	30th		nil	
	31st		70 OR proceeded Corps Concentration Camp for dismot.	

WAR DIARY or INTELLIGENCE SUMMARY

Army Form C. 2118.

Sheet III

Place	Date	Hour	Summary of Events and Information	Remarks and references to Appendices
TOURNAI	24th		nil	
	25th		70R proceeded to Corps Isolation Camp for demob and struck off strength. 2 OR proceeded to Étaples and struck off strength. 1/27 miles sent to base	
	26th		Battalion moved into billets at MARGUAIN. Passed 15 ORs marked killed 6/16-35/10. 1 OR in medical CCS & struck off strength	
MARGUAIN	27th		10 OR returned from leave and on duty list	
	28th		LT PKIMBER & 7 OR posted to 1st Bn. 166. 2 OR struck off strength. 1 OR struck off strength. Tempy Lt at Cookery School ÉTAPLES.	
	29th		From 6 RS and the following officers proceeded to join 1st Bn. 166. Today. Are struck off strength of Bn. LT (A/CAPT) WOOD G.W.A. LT (A/CAPT) TRENT W.A. MC. LT JCKNOTH LT H.E. PARSONS MC 2/LT A. LINLEY D.S. LAUGHLAND E.C. MORYOSEPH A.M. COOKE C.W. PETRIE MC	
	30th		nil	
	31st		7 OR proceeded to go Concentrate Camp for demob	

SECRET & CONFIDENTIAL.

VOLUME 13.

WAR DIARY FOR THE MONTH OF APRIL 1919.

[signature], Captain
Commanding 24th Battn. M.G.Corps.

Army Form C. 2118.

Instructions regarding War Diaries and Intelligence
Summaries are contained in F. S. Regs., Part II.
and the Staff Manual respectively. Title pages
will be prepared in manuscript.

WAR DIARY
or
INTELLIGENCE SUMMARY.
(Erase heading not required.)

Place	Date	Hour	Summary of Events and Information	Remarks and references to Appendices
MARGUAIN	APRIL	12ᵐ	20R ecacuated CCS + struck off strength. 30R reported from Base Depot and are taken on strength. 30R admitted to Military hospital	
	"	2ᵖᵐ	20R attacked Rw H7C9.	
	"	3ᵐ	10R returned from Div. Transport Park.	
	"	4ᵐ	Cache equipment inspected by Ordnance Board at BAPAUME at 1130 hrs.	
	"	5ᵐ	10R admitted F.A.	
	"	6ᵐ	10R struck off strength (in hospital 3 days) 1 OR wounded CCS + struck off strength.	
	"		1 OR handed over to 1ˢᵗ Bn. M.G.C.	
	"	7ᵐ	1 OR attacked Div. Sig. Cy. 10R identified return due to OC+ struck off strength # 15.2.19.	
	"	8ᵃ	30R joined from Div HQ + taken on strength.	
	"	9ᵐ	20 OR at Corps HQ returned + 20 cadre A men. 10R to Army Remt Officer struck off strength	
	"	10ᵐ	1 OR reported from CCS + taken on strength. 2/Lt. F.J. PHILLIPS returned from leave dated TOURNAI.	
	"	12ᵐ	Following Officers transferred to 1ˢᵗ Bn M.G.C. + taken off strength: Lt H. RODGERS, 2/Lt E.N.ESTHEAD, 2/Lt F.S. FRITH, 2/Lt E. FORD, 2/Lt F.J. PHILLIPS. 133 OR transferred to 5ᵗʰ Bn. M.G.C. + struck off strength.	

Army Form C. 2118.

WAR DIARY
or
INTELLIGENCE SUMMARY.
(Erase heading not required.)

Instructions regarding War Diaries and Intelligence Summaries are contained in F. S. Regs., Part II. and the Staff Manual respectively. Title pages will be prepared in manuscript.

Place	Date	Hour	Summary of Events and Information	Remarks and references to Appendices
MARQUAIN	APRIL 1st	12ⁿ	2OR evacuated CCS & struck off strength. 3OR reported from Base Depot and one taken on strength. 3OR admitted hospital	
	" 2nd		2OR attacked Bn 17/9.	
	" 3rd		1OR returned from Div Transport Pool.	
	" 4th		(rifle equipment suspected of Anthrax – Sent to Bailleul Road at 11:30 hrs.)	
	" 5th		1OR admitted F.A.	
	" 6th		1OR struck off strength (in hospital 1 day) 1OR evacuated CCS & struck off strength. 1OR transferred to 1st Bn MGC	
	" 7th		1OR attacked Aus Sqn 6/9. 1OR admitted [?] relation line to URs struck off 6/2 Bn A/5 2.19	
	" 8th		3OR joined from Aus MB & taken on strength	
	" 9th		20 OR at Corps HQ returned by 20 cadre X men 1OR to Army Records Officer struck off strength	
	" 10th		1OR reported from CCS & taken on strength. 2/Lt F.S. PHILLIPS returned from buffer duties TOURNAI	
	" 12th		Following Officers transferred to 1st Bn MGC & struck off strength. 2/Lt. A. RODGERS 2/Lt G.M. ESTHEAD, 2/Lt F.S. FRITH, 2/Lt E. FORD 2/Lt F.W. PHILLIPS O.S. 133 OR transferred to 5th Bn MGC & struck off strength.	

WAR DIARY or INTELLIGENCE SUMMARY

Army Form C. 2118.

(Erase heading not required.)

Place	Date	Hour	Summary of Events and Information	Remarks and references to Appendices
MARQUAIN	APRIL 13		Baths at Cache à Étangt.	
	14		4 offrs. + 12 OR visited YPRES battlefields.	
	16		A/Major C.G.C. GILBERT M.C. proceeded to concentration camp SOMAIN pro demob.	
	17		CAPT. H.H. ROBINSON M.C. proceeded on leave in France	
	18		2/Lt E.A. MOBBERLEY proceeded to join 33rd Bn. M.G.C. B.E.F. for duty. No attack off strength.	
	20		1 OR rejoined from CCS & taken on strength.	
	21		1 OR transferred to Class Z reserve whilst on leave to UK & struck off strength.	
	22		1 OR admitted hospital.	
			1 OR admitted CCS from hospital & struck off strength.	
	23		1 OR transferred to 5th Bn. M.G.C. & struck off strength. CAPT. H.H. ROBINSON M.C. returned from leave in FRANCE.	
	24		4 OR proceeded to UK for dis'n & are struck off strength.	
	27		1 OR reported from Base Depot & taken on strength.	
	29		2/Lt A.E. de R. NETHERAH D.S.O. M.C. proceeded on leave in France from 29.4.19 to 4.5.19. CAPT. H.H. ROBINSON M.C. assumes command of the cadre.	
	30		1 OR proceeded to 5th Bn M.G.C. & struck off strength. Lt. 8/Lt A. PICKEN proceeded to 11th Bn. M.G.C. for duty & struck off strength.	

Army Form C. 2118.

WAR DIARY
or
INTELLIGENCE SUMMARY.
(Erase heading not required.)

Instructions regarding War Diaries and Intelligence Summaries are contained in F. S. Regs., Part II. and the Staff Manual respectively. Title pages will be prepared in manuscript.

Place	Date	Hour	Summary of Events and Information	Remarks and references to Appendices
MARQUAIN	APRIL 13th		Baths at cache & fang R.	
	14th		L/offr & 12 OR visited YPRES battlefields	
	16th		Major C.G.C. GILBERT M.C. proceeded to concentration camp SOMAIN for demob.	
	17th		Capt. M.H. ROBINSON M.C. proceeded on leave in France	
	18th		2/Lt. E.A. MOBERLEY proceeded to join 33rd Bn M.G.C. B.E.F. for duty 1 O.R. struck off strength	
	20th		1 OR rejoined from CCS. taken on strength	
	21st		20 R transfered to Class Z Army reserve with-drawn leave to UK. struck off strength	
	22nd		1 OR admitted hospital	
	23rd		1 OR admitted CCS from hospital	
			1 OR transferred to 5th Bn M.G.C. struck off strength. Capt M.H. ROBINSON M.C. returned from leave in FRANCE	
	24th		4 OR proceeded to UK for duty & are struck off strength	
	27th		1 OR rejoined from leave beyond a Taken on strength	
	29th		Maj. A.E. or R. WETHERALL DSO MC proceeded on leave in France from 29.4.19 to 4.5.19. Capt M.H. ROBINSON MC assumed command of the units	
	30th		1 OR proceeded to 5th Bn M.G.C. struck off strength. Lt. G.J. A KILBEY proceeded to 41. Bn M.G.C. for duty & on strength	

Secret & confidential

Volume 14.

24TH BATTALION
MACHINE GUN
CORPS.

War Diary for Month of May 1919.

H.H. Robinson
Capt-adjt
24th Bn. M.G.C.

24th Div. Group.

Forwarded.

H.H. Robinson
Capt & adjt.
MG 678.
3/0/19. 24th Batt. M.G. Corps.

Army Form C. 2118.

WAR DIARY
or
INTELLIGENCE SUMMARY.
(Erase heading not required.)

Place	Date	Hour	Summary of Events and Information	Remarks and references to Appendices
MARQUAIN	MAY 1st		2 OR proceeded to Concentration Camp SOTRAIN for demob and are struck off strength	
	5th		3 OR proceeded to UK for duty & are struck off strength	
			Lt Col M E de R NETHERALL DSO MC returned from leave in France - 1 OR taken on strength in accordance with GRO 6685	
	8th		1 OR returned from CCS & taken on strength	
	12th		4 OR returned from Coffin Sulus Tournai	
	13th		Lieut E J G PALMER proceeded to join 1st Bn M.G.C. and is struck off strength	
	16th		1 OR admitted to Lees & struck off strength (Coy 248)	
	17th		1 OR returned from detachment	
	18th		1 OR posted to 58th Bn MGC from 1/5/19 & struck off strength	
	19th		2 OR reported from Corps HQ and are taken on strength	
	22nd		5 OR proceeded on escort duty to COLOGNE. 2 OR proceeded to join the 5th Bn M.G.C. and are struck off strength	
	23rd		1 OR reported from CCS & is taken on strength	
	25th		5 OR returned from escort duty to COLOGNE	

WAR DIARY
INTELLIGENCE SUMMARY

Army Form C. 2118.

Place	Date	Hour	Summary of Events and Information	Remarks and references to Appendices
MARQUAIN	May 28th	30th	CAPT. H.H. ROBINSON M.C. proceeded on leave in France (to 2/6/19) 10R admitted to Field Ambulance.	24/72.19.5C

www.ingramcontent.com/pod-product-compliance
Lightning Source LLC
Chambersburg PA
CBHW081540160426
43191CB00011B/1804